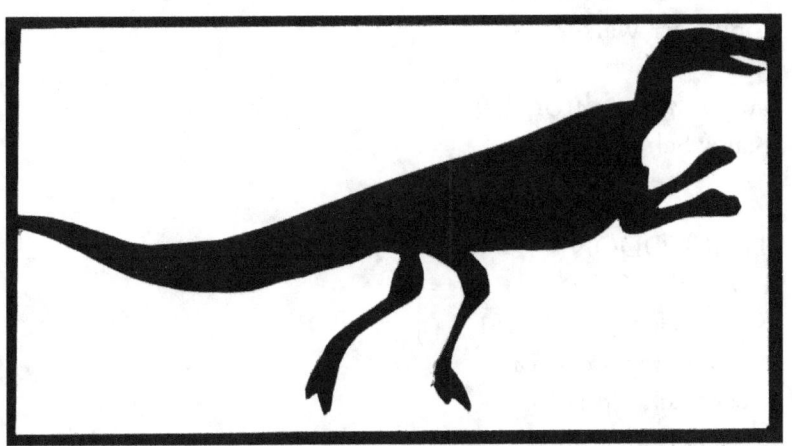

a dinosaur of a little magazine

I0553709

Issue 2, Spring 2011

Editor & Founder
John Carr Walker

Associate Editor
Katey Schultz

TRACHODON
PO Box 1468
Saint Helens, OR 97051
editor@trachodon.org
www.trachodon.org
www.cheekteethblog.com

TRACHODON welcomes submissions of fiction and nonfiction during the months of April-May and October-November online. Poetry is currently by invitation only; poets are free to query with a bio statement and description of work. Note that essays, articles, profiles, and other journalistic works should be about craft movements, antiquated processe or artisan culture. Nonfiction writers are encouraged to query first. Fiction may be any style on any theme or topic. Please read our expanded guidelines by visiting our website or maili us a stamped, self-addressed envelope.

Published twice yearly in paperback and ebook formats by Trachodon Publishing LLC.
Subscription rate: 2 issues (1 year) $18.
Canadian addresses add $3/issue, other international $6/issue.
Sample Issue $10. Canadian $13. Other international $16.
Ebooks are $4.99 per issue.
Limited backlist available. Please make checks payable to Trachodon Publishing LLC.
Visit our website for special offers, to place orders, and pay by credit card.

"Therapy" by Michael Delp originally appeared in the short story collection *As If We Were Prey* (Wayne State University Press, 2010).

Erratta: Jo Ann Heydron's story "Shoebox" was mistakenly listed as "Shoestring" on the cover of Issue 1. Our apologies to writer and readers.

ISSN: 2158-5970

Contents by Genre

Fiction

Nonfiction

Poetry

Photography

John Carr Walker

Editor's Note: Against Nostalgia

A friend remarked that what drew her to TRACHODON was our focus on nostalgia. It was meant as a compliment, and I took it as such, but that word *nostalgia* has been gnawing at me ever since.

I've always tried to avoid the bad company that profits on nostalgia. High School Reunions. *Dancing With the Stars*. Nicholas Sparks. Pulling out the family photo albums might make one feel nostalgic, but it's unlikely that snapshots of your vacation to Arches National Park will lead to the same explorations of emotional and psychological terrain as reading Edward Abbey.

My friend also happens to be very good writer. Exact diction is her habit and professional practice. This isn't a woman who slings words around unaware of their effects. Perhaps her comment was intended as a veiled question: "This Artisan Culture stuff, I mean, is it just an angle, or something more?" It took me months, but I realized that I didn't know the answer, even though I'd coined the phrase "artisan culture." The *nostalgia* label bothered me not because it was wrong, but because it might be correct.

Nothing ends a conversation quicker than tone. Aggressive tones can turn conversation into argument, and apologetic tones turn it into a simulacrum of conversation—something blanched, pussyfooting. The nostalgic tone ends the conversation in its tracks because the nostalgic self is stuck in a revelry that no one else can understand. As a literary device it's worthless because the best the reader can hope for is a thin companionship with the story—quite different from an emotional response I want the work in TRACHODON to create.

Without a doubt, nostalgia is a part of what we print. Many of the writers who've submitted write about the typewriter they inherited, or the leather-bound, hand-stitched Dickens library that their great-grandmother bought new—worthwhile topics both, but potentially dripping with nostalgia.

The writers we *publish* cut through the syrup. Nostalgia is the starting place, but never the end. We're taken through the static and the self-revelatory to something much more honest and moving. After all, an essay about a typewriter probably isn't about the machine, but about the person clacking the keys, the creative self that's unlocked by the physical act of composing on this instrument. Go there. Write about that. Objects are relatively simple, but identity is deeply complicated. Shannon Huffman Polson's essay later in this issue is an example of what can be exposed by drilling through the nostalgic layer to the core. And it's not an accident that the short stories and poems printed herein do precisely the same thing. Great writing never settles for a stroll down memory lane. Great writing repaves the damn road.

I'm immensely grateful to my very good writer friend for saying what she said about TRACHODON, as it's helped me address some of my blind spots as a publisher. Beginning with this issue, the dinosaur is publishing the magazine simultaneously as paperback and ebook. We'll soon be available through every major bookseller online and in brick-and-mortar stores. We've revamped our blog Cheek Teeth to feature articles by guest writers, more contributor profiles, and flash fiction (www.cheekteethblog.com). We're tweeting at twitter.com/trachodonmag, and our Facebook friends have doubled since the publication of Issue 1 in September of 2010.

Do I mean to suggest that traditional runs of print-only books are a nostalgic approach to publishing? Certainly not for everyone. For me, however, I realized that I was gazing a bit too lovingly at the way things were, while the ground under this dinosaur's feet was quickly turning to tar.

I'm a fan of the "little magazines" of the past. *STORY, The Little Review,* early *Partisan Review*—I've spent many happy hours searching the shelves of used bookstores for old issues, though the search is almost always fruitless. I'm able to indulge my nostalgic fondness for these artifacts precisely because they are artifacts, relics of the past. And yet taking the nostalgic view of TRACHODON would have me believe that our method of publication is more important than what we publish. As a literary journal, we are a conduit, and it doesn't matter whether we're being read on a screen or between paperback covers, if we're stored on a device or on a shelf or in a back pocket. So long as we're available to as many readers as possible, we're fulfilling our mission.

I wonder sometimes what went through editor Whit Burnett's mind as he mimeographed the first issue of *STORY* in 1931. Did he wonder if he was choosing the right printing method? Should he have had the magazine printed by a professional shop using moveable type instead of this derided new contraption? Burnett would go on to publish to some of the most recognizable names in literature, launching quite a few careers along the way. Given the quality of writing it featured, it's easy to forget that *STORY* used new technology to produce an inexpensive book, which in turn allowed Burnett to introduce writers such as Anton Chekhov, J.D. Salinger, and William Saroyan to far more readers.

Indeed, praises be for very good writer friends.

Scott Nadelson

FORKED RIVER

Ellie had been with men before. Until she was twenty-three she'd been with men exclusively, nearly a dozen of them, and then three more interspersed among her first experiments with women the year after she graduated from NYU. That was her radical year, when she moved from Park Slope to Jersey City, when she joined Solidarity and learned to drive a forklift, when she had a nipple pierced and a union logo tattooed on her left shoulder blade. Even going to bed with men had seemed radical at the time, at least the men she found herself with—a scruffy labor organizer, an emaciated drummer in a methadone program, a married longshoreman.

Sleeping with women had felt safe by contrast, and infinitely more pleasurable. Even the toughest butch girls, the ones with self-made scars on their arms and legs, the ones who rode motorcycles and talked about strippers and bar fights, the ones who threatened to do themselves or Ellie harm if she went through with leaving them as she said she would, all had a comfortable predictability about them, a familiar softness that was easy to detect beneath hardened exteriors, a tide of emotions she could drift upon, no matter how erratic its ebb and flow. She was never surprised by women the way she was by men, who could turn their anger on her without warning, or suddenly go weepy and declare their tormented love, whose affection so often seemed to wax and wane with the blood flowing into and out of their cocks.

Predictability was what she had with Val, for the most part, though they'd had their share of surprises during the past six years: the sudden heart attack that killed Ellie's father; the ex-girlfriend who showed up unexpectedly and sent Val into the first serious depression she'd suffered since college; the burst pipes that flooded their old apartment and destroyed their books and clothes and stereo. Val was moody and overly sensitive and always picked fights with Ellie after getting off the phone with her mother, but she was also consistently tidy and thoughtful, making dinner those nights Ellie worked late, bringing home new placemats or a throw rug or a set of scented candles with every paycheck. She'd covered most of their rent for the two years Ellie had been in graduate school and hadn't complained once, not even during the months when Ellie disappeared almost entirely into the writing of her master's thesis, an analysis of the labor movement's failures in western New Jersey and eastern Pennsylvania.

Val's presence in bed—her expanding backside, her shoulders still strong from years of swimming, her warm, hissing breath—had become such a fixture in Ellie's life that she had trouble sleeping those nights they were apart, when she had to stay in Trenton during important legislative sessions. Their lovemaking had become infrequent but still had plenty of fire to it, always leaving Ellie with the feeling of having jumped off a cliff and survived.

Ten years had passed since she'd first discovered that feeling, with an Israeli girl who'd picked her up at a club downtown and took her to an Alphabet City apartment she shared with four other women. The girl was chatty on the walk over, talking about clubs and music and slam poetry, but as soon as they got into the bedroom she was silent. She went about taking off Ellie's clothes in an expert, studied way, but her attentions to Ellie's body were careless, casual, earth-shaking. Afterward she said, regretfully, "That was your first time. So you'll always remember me."

Ellie was so astonished to realize what she'd been missing that she didn't notice until two days later that the girl had stolen her credit card and charged three hundred dollars at K-Mart. She was furious, but also strangely excited, and then finally dumbstruck when she saw the list of purchases: underwear and bras, cough syrup, a clock radio, a coffee maker, sponges and dish soap, laundry detergent, shoelaces, envelopes, drill bits. How could something so passionate, something so new and unexpected, come to such a terribly mundane end?

~

At thirty-three, Ellie didn't think much about passion anymore. She had no time for it. She worked as a lobbyist for the state employees' union, with a reputation in the capital for quiet resolve and dignity, a reputation earned during her first session four years ago, when she'd testified about salary inequity before a hostile Assembly committee. A bill scheduled to come to the floor would have meant a huge pay cut for workers in social service agencies, primarily women. For nearly two hours she'd stood up to the bullying of half a dozen Republican legislators, one of whom, to her utter disbelief, called her a femi-fascist—did he mean femi-Nazi?—and asked how long she'd been studying the works of Karl Marx. "You wouldn't be complaining," he said, "if you had a man at home bringing in the big bucks. But then, you don't go in for men, do you?"

She maintained her composure, answering firmly that her sexual orientation was irrelevant to a discussion of workers' rights. "And if I'm not mistaken," she added, "your wife earns quite a bit more than you do, doesn't she, Assemblyman? Nearly double? Shouldn't our public employees have the same opportunity?"

Afterward she spent twenty minutes weeping in a toilet stall, ready to quit, ready to abandon the movement altogether, so clearly a lost cause. But over the next few days she had people coming up to congratulate her: co-workers, aides to several Democrats, a reporter from the *Star Ledger*. A fellow lobbyist from the airline industry bought her lunch in the State House cafeteria the following week, called her a tough kid, and tried to hire her away from the union.

And then she was invited to visit the office of the assemblyman who'd insulted her. Ham Wheeler. He'd just been elected to his seventh term in Sussex County and had seniority on two of his three committees. He was lean except for a bulging belly, with dark oiled hair parted crisply on the left and a big, bumpy nose more Semitic than any in Ellie's family. Reading glasses softened his jowly look and gave him a kindly, paternal appearance that was hard to connect with the blustery way he strutted on the Assembly floor. He was in his mid-fifties, roughly the same age as Ellie's father, whose funeral she'd attended less than four months earlier. She didn't want to see her father in Ham Wheeler, but the two men shared similar politics, Ellie's father a contractor who'd squabbled with unions his entire life. He'd been delighted when she'd moved back to Jersey, though he couldn't understand why she'd want to be in the middle of that urban mess of Hudson County, when the houses were so much bigger and more comfortable in the suburbs where she'd grown up, the schools better, the streets safer. Then, after she came out, he didn't speak to her for a year, and even after they reconciled, always referred to Val as her roommate.

Ham Wheeler smiled and gazed at her over his glasses when she came in, and she was aware of pulling herself to full height, widening her stance. "Miss Schatz," he said. "So nice to see you. Please, have a seat."

As much as Ellie tried for an androgynous look, keeping her hair short and stylishly spiky, her suits cut loosely over her curves, she had a sprightly femininity she couldn't hide; it drew constant condescension, from men and women alike. She was short and slender, with little hands and feet, her jaw sleek, chin pointed, skin milky. Her voice had a squeaky quality she hated and tried to make up for by exaggerating her Jersey accent, an approximation of her father's. She stood in front of Ham Wheeler, reluctant to take the chair he offered, which would have given him the opportunity to look down on her. On his desk was a copy of *The Maltese Falcon*, and on the wall behind his chair a framed photograph of Humphrey Bogart holding the black bird.

"Hammett," he said, and she felt herself flush, realizing he'd followed her gaze, ashamed to know how much her eyes gave away. "My full name." His father was a fan of hard-boiled crime novels of the thirties and forties, he said. He had a sister, Chan, short for Chandler, and a brother, Cain, named not for the Biblical murderer, nor the author of *The Postman Always Rings Twice*, but for Paul Cain, whose novel *Fast One* was his father's favorite. "All blood and guts and backstabbing gangsters," Wheeler said. "Probably not your cup of tea."

"I didn't mean to barge in," she said. "I stopped by to make an appointment, but your secretary—"

"My assistant," he said, and smiled his fatherly smile.

"She told me to come on in. But if you're busy—"

"Please, Miss Schatz," he said. "Sit already. And stop apologizing. I'm the one who should be apologizing to you."

"There's no need," she said. She eased into the chair, smoothing her slacks and pulling her jacket tight around her shoulders. But even looking down on her, Ham Wheeler's expression was surprisingly gentle. She read concern, even, in the arch of his eyebrows and the way he tented his hands.

"I've got nothing against you or your sort," he said. "I want you to know that." He rapped knuckles on the desk and jerked back in his chair. "I'll even let you in on a secret. My sister's a lesbian." His face altered as he said that last word, nose crinkling as if he smelled something rotten. The last thing Ellie's father had said to her before he'd had the coronary, words that had haunted the most unexpected moments of the past four months, struck her again now: "Isn't it bad enough not to have a normal kid? Do you have to announce it to the whole world?" They'd been fighting about the commitment ceremony she and Val had been planning for the following summer, which he refused to help pay for and swore he wouldn't attend. She'd hung up on him, and two days later he was gone. "Not many people know that," Wheeler went on. "You could use it against me out on the floor if you want. But I don't think you will. It's my peace offering. Something to build our trust on."

"And why shouldn't I use it? Why should you trust me?"

"I've got no choice," he said. "You've blocked my bill. You

really lit a fire under my friends on the other side of the aisle. So now we work together." He told her his plan. A compromise bill, one the union could live with. She'd back its passage, and most of the lefties would fall into line. It wasn't perfect, not for either of them. But what in life was? "Well done, Miss Schatz," he said as she rose and shook his hand. "That's some fine lobbying. And you should know, my wife was thrilled to hear she'd finally gotten some credit. All these years of supporting me and never a moment of glory."

"It's been a pleasure, Assemblyman," she said.

"Ham," he said, and winked. "*Treyf* your people call it, right, Miss Schatz? I ain't too kosher."

"Good on sandwiches, though," she said, and was conscious of swinging her hips on the way out of his office, conscious of his eyes on her. She stopped at his door, turned, and said, "Give my best to your wife and sister. And if you want, call me Ellie."

~

In four years she'd worked to block half a dozen more bills and helped push two of the union's own through the Assembly, another three through the Senate. She had a knack for compromise, though at times she wondered if she'd compromised away everything she had, her convictions, her values, her drive. The state employees were no better off than before, but her own salary had risen steadily, and after the burst pipe she and Val traded up apartments, leaving Jersey City for Weehawken, a building on the Palisades, with a partial view of Midtown. "Next move we're going across the river," Val said. "Enough of this halfway stuff."

Most of the time Ellie had her back to Manhattan, in her Newark office or driving from one corner of the state to another. New Jersey felt more like home now than it ever had when she was growing up, though her father had always tried to instill in her his pride in the state—the topography was more varied than New York's, he'd said, and the people had more character. Her mother couldn't wait to get back to the city of her youth, selling the house and moving into a co-op in Chelsea within a year of the funeral. The city held less mystery for Ellie now than did the strange towns she drove to along the shore, or around the edges of the Pine Barrens, or at the north end of the Delaware Water Gap. After chatting with workers at hospitals, at construction sites, at DMV offices, the glitz of Manhattan felt less real to her, far less compelling. But Val had only recently struggled her way out of the depression that had so suddenly knocked her off her feet, and to keep her cheerful, Ellie agreed that one day they'd make the leap. "I'll leave this labor mess behind," she said. "Workers are screwed no matter what I do."

In her heart she wasn't yet ready to give up. The union was working on a new contract, its first real shot at parity, and a comprehensive overhaul of the state's benefit package. Ellie had been charged with lobbying the recently elected Assembly members, particularly Republicans. She had several allies on the right now. Ham Wheeler was the most consistent, always finding a way to back her and still please the industry friends who bankrolled his campaigns, all of which he'd won with little challenge. She'd had dinner with him and his wife, had met his lesbian sister, had spent an afternoon on his boat off Cape May. She sent birthday cards to all his children and brought him a bottle of single malt Scotch every Christmas, the brand her father had raved about after coming home from a golfing trip to Saint Andrews.

Wheeler was planning a run for Congress in a year, and Ellie promised him union support if he helped get the contract passed before leaving the Assembly. He gave her a list of new members he thought might be pliable and greased the wheel as much as he could. But he made no promises. "Some of these folks'll go running as soon as they see you," he said. "Liberal dyke Jew. Three strikes against you right there."

"But when you say it, it sounds so charming," Ellie said.

~

Jordan Gearhart was the new assemblyman from District 9,

with an office in Forked River. He was twenty-seven, a former college football star and Army lieutenant, now chief financial officer of his father's salvage firm. He'd surprised everyone in Trenton by taking on and beating a three-term incumbent in the primary, running on a homeland security platform that had as its centerpiece the fear of terrorists sneaking onto the beaches of Ocean County. Ellie didn't think she had much chance with Gearhart and wouldn't have bothered with him at all if Ham Wheeler hadn't encouraged her, saying, "He's just a kid. He doesn't know what he's doing. You might convince him the contract'll keep the terrorists out of Barnegat Bay." Then, with a wink, he added, "Wouldn't hurt if you showed him some skin, too. Army boys. You know how they are."

The photos on his campaign Web site showed Gearhart as a wholesome family man, with two daughters, ages two and four, and a lovely, slim-hipped wife in a modest dress and modest heels, blonde curls piled high on her head. Gearhart had sandy hair parted over his blocky forehead, sharp green eyes, a square chin, a corded neck. His posture was straight but naturally so, his smile easy and lacking any hint of self-consciousness. Fundamentalist, Ellie guessed. Or frat boy. Or both. Someone who felt he should be looked at—by other people, by God—and universally admired.

In person, the impression at first only deepened. He was overly solicitous when she visited his district office, stepping out from behind his desk to shake her hand, pulling out a chair and holding it until she'd sat, offering her coffee or tea or a mint from an overflowing bowl on his sideboard. His office was a parody of a politician's office, something he might have set up after watching an episode of *The West Wing*. The U.S. and state flags hung on either side of the window, both poles topped with silver eagles in flight. Over his desk were two framed portraits, one of George Washington, one of George W. Bush. The bookshelf was filled with texts from Civics 101, the Constitution, the Federalist Papers, the Autobiography of Benjamin Franklin, held up on either side by busts of the founding fathers. There was no Bible in sight, and that gave Ellie hope. She hadn't taken Wheeler's advice, wearing a suit and sensible shoes, her blouse buttoned almost to her neck.

And maybe it had been a mistake. After he'd settled her in, Gearhart's gaze drifted past her shoulder as she spoke about her bill, its likely boost to the state's economy, its necessity for keeping services running efficiently. She hoped to catch his attention by talking about state trooper salaries and the impact on security, but he held the same disinterested expression, his chair swiveled forty-five degrees away from her, so that his profile lined up with George Washington's. She thought he'd be impressed when she told him which of his colleagues had pledged their support to the union, but names didn't faze him, not even Ham Wheeler's. With surprisingly delicate fingers, he twirled a pen beside his ear whenever she paused to take a breath. There was something distasteful about his face, she decided. His lips were pale and thin but strangely moist and slightly parted. They were unseemly with his high cheekbones and bulging Adam's apple, something raw and naked about them that distracted her and made her less articulate than she would have liked. His eyes, eager when she'd come in, had gone sleepy and half-lidded. When she finished her pitch, he opened them, turned to face her, and flushed deeply. "You don't … seem to be," he said, stammering, gesturing with his pen toward her lap. "It's surprising."

"Excuse me?"

"Married," he said. "You don't seem to be married." He jabbed his pen again, and she looked down at her legs crossed in loose black slacks, wondering what it was he saw there that gave her away. "No ring," he said. "It's just … hard to believe, that's all."

She laughed without meaning to. What had she thought he'd been looking at? Her virginal crotch? He laughed with her, nervously, and she waved a hand in front of her face. "Excuse me," she said. "I'm not laughing at you. You just caught me off guard."

"I shouldn't have asked," he said. "It wasn't right. I don't usually get so personal. It's just—"

"I do hope we can count on your support," Ellie said, working to control her laughter, which now simmered silently in her chest, a threatening hilarity from which, once let loose, she might not recover. "For the contract, I mean."

He flipped the pen in the air, caught it, and smacked it twice on the desk. His eyes blinked away the distracting thought. "I'll consult my constituents," he said impatiently.

"That's all I ask."

He glanced over his shoulder, out the window, and when he turned back his face was composed again, as eager as it had been when she'd first arrived. "It's getting late," he said. "Maybe you'd like to talk more about your…thing …over a drink? Or dinner?"

She was used to being hit on by legislators and their aides, by union members and fellow lobbyists, plenty of them married, and normally she was quick with a brush-off that was firm but compassionate, that made her seem flattered but definitively uninterested, playful enough not to cause offense. Once, a senator from Edison, old enough to be her grandfather, now, thankfully, retired, had pulled her aside at a fundraiser, bent close to her ear, and whispered, "I'd fuck you into next week." Without hesitation, even as his wine-soured breath lingered in her nose, she replied, "I'd hate to miss the weekend. Thanks anyway, Senator," and he gave her an affectionate pat on the back before stumbling away. To Gearhart she might have said, *Shouldn't you ask your wife first?* or *Only if I can bring my girlfriend along.* But for some reason she was flummoxed by the way his eyes were fixed on her, those wet lips more suggestive and inappropriate than what he'd proposed, his eager smile turning rigid and desperate the longer she hesitated. There was an innocence about him that made her want to be gentle. His wide shoulders leaned the slightest bit toward her, corded neck straining against collar and tie. His square chin was only inches from a photo of his family on the beach—facing outward on the desk, toward visitors—all of them in shorts and

T-shirts, a wave crashing behind them. She thanked him and apologized and mentioned the long drive she had ahead of her. "Another time," she said.

He leaned back in his chair, relieved and confident, once again the frat boy she'd first imagined. "Of course," he said, standing, arms wide to usher her out. "I understand." He held the door for her and then walked her through the outer office, empty now of aides and assistants, out of the building, all the way to the parking lot, delivering the entire time what sounded like a stump speech, about his service to his country, about the need to protect the state's citizens from every threat, about his determination to cut taxes and spur growth along the mid-shore. He didn't stammer at all now. Then, standing beside her Saturn plastered with bumper stickers—union slogans, Kerry/Edwards '04, a pair of rainbows—he suddenly jammed his hands into his pockets and looked up at the overcast sky. "I can't believe it," he said.

"Can't believe what?"

"That you just walked into my office, like anybody else."

"Assemblyman—"

"It's so unexpected, isn't it? Going along with ordinary life, and then out of nowhere…"

A breeze brought the salty, rotten smell of the marshes and the Waterway, and a trio of seagulls wheeled overhead. She swallowed and cleared her throat and adjusted the briefcase on her shoulder. It was time to put an end to this, but again the words got stuck in her mouth, and now it was she who found herself stammering. "I do hope you'll take our bill seriously. It's not only good for our employees, but for the entire—"

"I'll hold you to that dinner," he said, turning abruptly and hurrying away. "Don't think I'll forget."

~

Ellie and Val had never had their commitment ceremony. They'd canceled it after Ellie's father's funeral and hadn't rescheduled. No matter how much time had passed, Ellie worried that she wouldn't make it through her vows without hearing her father's final words and fighting off the anger they stirred, along with the exasperating guilt she knew she had no reason to indulge. And anyway, she and Val were as committed as they needed to be. They had a shared lease, joint ownership of the car, insurance in both their names. They'd drawn up living wills, putting each other in charge of hospital care and medical decisions, both refusing resuscitation and feeding tubes. Ellie hadn't worn rings for years now—driving so much, her fingers always swelled on the steering wheel and she didn't want anything binding them. Even if she and Val had gone through with exchanging rings, she wouldn't have worn hers to work, and Gearhart would have jumped to the same conclusion. She used to joke that she'd tattoo Val's name on her arm, but her tattooing days were over, and if anything she wanted the one she had—faded now, an embarrassing reminder of how naïve she'd once been, how bright-eyed and hopeful— surgically removed.

She had every intention of telling Val about her strange encounter with the new assemblyman, to shake her head over the absurdities of her job and the ridiculous straight people she had to deal with. She would have feigned outrage, saying that if it weren't for the bill she would have gotten right on the phone with the union's lawyer, with the chair of the Joint Committee on Ethical Standards. She would have left out the giggling that finally overtook her on the drive home, stuck in traffic on the Parkway, which gummed up near Matawan and crept around an accident outside South Amboy. Why did Gearhart's words amuse her so much? Why did the thought of his earnest face send her into fits of laughter? It was more than flattery, she thought. It was plain comedy. But she didn't know how she'd explain this to Val, who'd certainly be outraged on her behalf, encouraging her to take action, and by the time she made it home, an hour later than she'd planned, she'd decided against saying anything at all.

And as soon as she opened the door to the apartment, she knew that talking wasn't an option anyway. Dishes were piled in the sink, a pot of cold pasta on the stove. Val was at the living room window, staring out at the lights of Midtown, and Ellie understood at once that she'd have to keep quiet. It was one of Val's fragile moments. She could read the signs in the way Val perched against the corner of the sofa, in the way she held her wine glass, curled beneath her chin. The wrong word might make her lash out, accuse Ellie of coming home late on purpose, of ruining their dinner—or worse, it might start her crying, making her question once again why nothing seemed to have meaning, why her life had no purpose.

These moments had become scattered now, and Ellie had learned to let them pass without calling attention to them, pretending not to notice anything was wrong—at best she could expect an evening of brooding silence and heavy sighs. Val was thirty-seven, short and growing plump, with speckles of gray in her dark hair. Most days she was bold enough to put on outrageous costume jewelry with her business suits, and in the past few years she'd taken to wearing vintage hats from the '20s and '30s, always acting surprised when they brought her compliments. She had a law degree, and had once worked exclusively for non-profits, though by the time Ellie met her she'd given up progressive causes and terrible pay for the perks of the corporate world.

To Ellie's mind, Val's job was the real problem. What meaning could she find in handling permissions and copyright infringements for a magazine conglomerate, sitting all day in a sterile office around the corner from Bryant Park? But Val rarely complained about work and would have gone on happily enough, it seemed, if the ex-girlfriend, Jean, hadn't appeared without warning two years ago, throwing everything into confusion. For Jean, the encounter was nothing but casual. She'd been passing through New York, she'd thought of Val and looked her up, she suggested meeting for lunch. More than ten years had passed since they'd broken up, and Jean had transformed—as had Val—from an angry punk rocker into a mild-mannered woman approaching middle age. The lunch was perfectly pleasant. Jean was living in

Vermont, her partner was pregnant, they were thinking about buying a four-acre hobby farm at the end of a gravel road. But it was precisely this pleasantness that knocked Val off her center. "She was so *cruel* when we were together," she said that night, her chest heaving with sobs. "She once threw a fucking *chair* at me. And now she can pretend we're old friends? She can forget any of it happened?"

"People change," Ellie told her. "She's not the same person she was then."

But this was the worst thing she could have said. For the next few days Val looked at her as if she might suddenly become unrecognizable, a total stranger. Ellie found herself checking the mirror more often than usual, and of course there *had* been changes since she and Val had first met—her skin was finally free of blemishes, her cheeks had lost their babyish roundness, her hair had returned to its natural color after years of bleaching and dyeing. She looked better than she ever had. But she couldn't convince Val that she could count on her, that certain things were solid no matter what. She didn't know if she really believed it herself, not after the planes flew into the Twin Towers, not after her father's heart attack. But for Val's sake, she said it as sincerely as she could. By the weekend, though, Val could hardly get out of bed, and since then she'd lived her life as if at any moment the air she breathed would suddenly turn to poison.

Tonight, all the lights in the apartment were off but the kitchen's. Val didn't turn around when Ellie closed the door. "Sorry I'm late," Ellie said, putting on a weary, disgruntled voice, trying to cover the giddy cheerfulness she'd felt on the drive home. "Awful jam at Exit 125."

Val didn't answer. She took a sip of wine. Ellie set her briefcase on the floor and joined her. Another apartment building blocked their view to the right, so they could see only from the Chrysler Building up to the 59th Street pier. She preferred this view to the one south, where the altered skyline still startled her, even five years later. Her father used to take her to the top of a hill half a mile from their house, and on a clear day they'd been able to glimpse the towers shimmering on the horizon. The buildings had always seemed mirage-like to Ellie as a girl, not entirely real, and now she sometimes thought they'd turned out to be a mirage after all. The tragedy had shaken her father, more deeply than she could have imagined. It wasn't so much that the towers had been attacked that shocked him, but that they'd collapsed so easily. "What were they built out of?" he said the next day, his voice trembling. "Lincoln Logs?" For a month afterward he called Ellie every day, just to hear her voice, she suspected, asking how the air was in her part of the state, if she could still smell the smoke.

"Let's go look for a place this weekend," Val said finally, her voice muted by the rim of the wine glass.

"Sure," Ellie said, trying to sound agreeable but noncommittal, trying not to provoke an argument. "Maybe Sunday. I've got to go into the office on Saturday."

"I heard about a building on Amsterdam, in the Seventies. Spacious for the rent."

"We'll check it out."

"If it's nice we should jump on it."

"Our lease isn't up for four months," Ellie said carefully. "We can't afford to lose the deposit." But this was pushing too hard. Val's shoulders stiffened. She drained the last of her wine. Ellie should have known better, she should have played along. "We'll check it out anyway."

It was too late. A trembling started in Val's chin, and a moment later her face crumpled. "I wouldn't feel so awful if I didn't have to cross that damn river every day," she said against Ellie's neck when she could gather enough breath to speak. "This place is killing me."

"I know," Ellie said, though she'd always been skeptical that moving would make any difference. How would a change of location give Val any more purpose than she had now? How would it make her any more certain about the world? "We'll do it as soon as it's the right time."

"Promise?"

The view here was too busy, she thought, garish and mesmerizing. Other places in the state appealed to her more now than they ever had before—the pine and oak forests to the south, the cultivated hills to the west, the tall grasses of the waterway, the boardwalks and sand and waves. And with the thought of beaches came Jordan Gearhart's face, ardent as a zealot's, followed by a great bubble of laughter rising to her throat. She cut it off by coughing. "You won't always feel this way," she said. "Things will get easier."

"You keep saying that," Val said. "But it's never true."

~

She didn't see Gearhart again until the end of the month, at the start of the new legislative session. It was her first time back in Trenton since the previous spring, and as always it surprised her to find how important she felt walking beneath the State House's double-tiered pillars, to gaze at the inside of the dome, with its gold balcony railings and scarlet walls hung with oil paintings of long-dead statesmen. The feeling would pass soon enough, she knew—all it took was a single session, an hour of bloated speeches, and the place quickly lost its dignity and grace. From the gallery she spotted Gearhart among his Republican colleagues, wearing that bored, impatient expression, scratching at his thumbnail with a pen as the Speaker announced the business of the day. She was surprised to realize how much she'd anticipated seeing him again, expecting a return of her giddiness, a guilty little thrill, and was even more surprised to find herself disappointed. She'd somehow forgotten how bulky his body was, how square his face, how stiff the wave of sandy hair swooping over his broad forehead. In the intervening weeks she'd formed an image of him in her mind that was smaller, softer-looking, less squeaky-clean. An idle fantasy to distract her from anxieties at work, she'd told herself, one she'd now have to let go.

Ellie planned to be in the capital all month, staying at a motel on Route 1. It was the last big push, she told Val, and after this was over she'd be home for at least half a year. They could take a vacation. They could look for a place in the city. The union contract would go to committee in the next few days, and unless something went awry, would come to the Assembly floor for debate in another week. Eight months of work, and still she was feeling doubtful. She'd gotten a commitment from four new members, and another two were on the fence, waiting to see which way the wind blew. But most had been like Gearhart, politely disinterested and dismissive. Ham Wheeler told her not to worry—he was working behind the scenes, building coalitions. It was what he did best. But Wheeler had already announced his candidacy for Congress and had one foot out of the State House. In her conversations over the last month she'd already sensed his influence dwindling.

Nerves didn't help her sleep that first night. Nor did the unpleasant discovery that she was sharing a floor of her motel with a pair of girls' soccer teams, in town for a three-day tournament. Concern about Val's mood already had her jittery—a whole month without Ellie's caretaking, and she might tip into some ravine of despair from which she couldn't climb out. The motel bed was wide and empty, the mattress sagging, the sheets smelling of starch and old cigarettes. All night there were doors slamming, girls squealing, footsteps drumming down the hallway. Ellie dozed for two hours, woke sweating and dehydrated, studied her notes for another three, and then lay in the dark staring at the ceiling. When she called home in the morning, groggy and mildly nauseous, Val sounded chipper, telling her about a phone call from her sister, and an interaction with her boss, and the fresh bok choy she'd bought at the Whole Foods near Lincoln Center. "If we lived in the city, we could shop there every day," she said.

"You sound good," Ellie said, a little doubtfully, not wanting to test her luck. "Did you call Dr. Gershenhorn?"

"Sometimes," Val said, "it's easier when you're not here."

"Oh?"

"If I get mopey, and no one's around to listen, I just have to tell myself to get over it. And usually I do."

"Great," Ellie said, furious, trying to cover her anger by forcing a laugh. "Next time I'm home you can pretend I'm deaf."

She had three cups of coffee before lunch, but still she couldn't shake the fog of exhaustion that settled over her, making her thoughts sluggish and strained. Her vision seemed grainy, nothing quite in focus, and she was quickly irritated by the two male colleagues she joined in line at the cafeteria, one from her own union, the other from the AFL-CIO. Both bemoaned the difficulty of their cause, their anticipated failures. Whiners, she thought. Why take these jobs if they weren't willing to fight? She was hungry, but the sight of food turned her stomach, and she took only a salad and breadstick. She fumbled with her purse, trying to find change for the impatient cashier—non-union, underpaid, no benefits—when a twenty-dollar bill slipped in front of her and a voice said, close to her ear, "Eleanor. Let me take care of this."

There was Gearhart standing beside her, his sharp eyes and square chin, those wet, parted lips. His suit looked strange on his wide shoulders and narrow waist, an oversized costume, though it had been tailored to fit perfectly. "Thank you, Assemblyman, I've got it," she said, still rummaging, but the cashier snatched Gearhart's bill and handed him change.

No one called her Eleanor, not even her mother, after whose great aunt Ellie had been named. No one but her paternal grandparents, both long dead. Her business card read Ellie, and so did her State House badge.

"I hope you'll join me," he said, flushing, his voice strained, a strong hand on her back, guiding her forward. "I've been thinking about you…about your bill. I need to hear more of the details… to understand what I'd be supporting…"

She caught looks from her colleagues, one raising an eyebrow. Across the cafeteria Ham Wheeler, surrounded by beefy men who shared his affection for boats and cigars and tax breaks, smiled a bemused, curious smile. She let Gearhart lead her to a table in the corner, where he held a chair for her until she sat. He took off his jacket and rolled his sleeves, his forearms as thick as her calves, bulging with muscle, artificial-looking next to his slender fingers. "I'm glad you're thinking about supporting us," she said, and went into her usual pitch, explaining how the contract would put more money into the hands of the state's consumers, boosting both the economy and tax revenues. "It's good for everyone," she said, but if he thought so too he didn't show it. He was studying the veins on the backs of his hands, his thumbs drumming the table. One nail was blue where he'd colored it in during the previous day's session.

"I was thinking," he said after a while, his eyes lifting slowly, "I was thinking, maybe, we could go across to Philly. Hit one of the steak joints everyone talks about."

She couldn't decide which was more genuine, the boyish shyness in his voice or the confident smile that followed, that suggested he always got what he wanted and expected that trend to continue. "Really, Assemblyman, I'm flattered—"

"I hear the Capital Grille isn't bad," he said. "Everyone says Morton's, but who wants to go to Philly for a Chicago steak?"

"—and if this is just professional, I'd be happy to meet with you anytime…dinner, or…I could bring one of my colleagues along—"

"I'll find a place," he said, and his smile began to slip, those damp lips growing almost pouty. "A quiet place. Out of the way. Where we can get to know each other."

"Assemblyman. You're married."

He leaned back and yanked on his tie. "Jordan," he said. "My friends call me Jordie. Or J-Dog." She burst out laughing. She couldn't help herself. A few tables away, her union colleagues glanced over, both looking despondent, shoulders hunched, their plates smeared with ketchup. Quitters, she thought. Gearhart's smile returned, uneasily, and he leaned toward her again. "Best steak in Philly, on me."

"I'm a vegetarian," she said, still laughing despite herself, aware of how her face reddened when she did, how young she sounded and frivolous.

"Ah," he said. "That explains it."

"Explains what?"

"Why you've got such a great figure."

She made herself stop laughing and shook her head. "Really, Assemblyman, this isn't appropriate at all. You're married and I—"

"Just professional," he said in a hurry, the smile entirely cracked now, nearly a grimace. "A working relationship. There's nothing wrong with us being sociable, is there?"

"And you're going to support our contract?"

"Well," he said. "My constituents—"

"If we're going to have a working relationship," she said, "we've got to have something to work on."

"I'm still thinking about it," he said.

"Have you even read the bill?"

"I need more time with it," he said, looking down at his hands again, and again Ellie thought his clothes looked strange on his bulky body, or else his body looked strangely stuffed beneath them, a sculpted balloon. "I need to study it a bit more." He seemed fragile as a balloon, too, easily deflated, his self-assurance fading now, replaced by a doubtful scrunching of his forehead, an attempt to look serious. She finally turned her attention to her salad, ravenous after all the talk of steaks, and ate silently, forking leaves into her mouth, crunching slowly, looking at Gearhart only occasionally. "Maybe if you can walk me through it, I'll be able to understand it better," he said.

"Don't you two look friendly." It was Ham Wheeler's voice—not the gentle, fatherly one he used in private, but his performance voice, blustery and condescending, the one that dominated the Assembly floor. He was in his performance stance as well, hands on hips, head cocked to the side, looking down at them from the end of the table. "Risky territory for a Freshman," he said to Gearhart. "In bed with the enemy. You'd better watch out,

Assemblyman."

"I'm not…" Gearhart stammered. "We're just…"

"Nothing more dangerous than a good-looking Marxist," Wheeler said. "Even if she doesn't swing our way."

"Excuse me?" Gearhart said. He squinted, perplexed, and then half-stood, with a threatening look, as if Wheeler had insulted him. Ellie faked a laugh, furious with Wheeler for stepping in when he had—couldn't he see she was trying to land a vote?—and after a second Wheeler read her expression and joined in. Gearhart did too, tentatively, looking back and forth between them, and Ellie was struck again by the vulgarity of his lips, fleshy and wet and too pale for the tan skin around them. Ham Wheeler was sweating, his forehead shining in the glare of the cafeteria's tube lighting. She stood, abandoning her salad despite her hunger.

"Mr. Wheeler and I go back a long way," she said to Gearhart, who looked pained again and lost. "I'm fast friends with anyone who does good things for my union." To Wheeler she said, "I'll walk with you, Assemblyman, if you don't mind. Are you heading back to the chamber?"

She caught a hint of Gearhart's smell as she passed him, a muskiness mixed with something artificially sweet, some kind of deodorant, maybe, or hair product, though what it reminded her of most was baby powder. She avoided eye contact but then glanced back from the doorway. He was watching her, sitting alone at his table, no food in front of him. He had no business here, she thought. Not in the cafeteria, not in the State House, not with her. She was embarrassed for him, and suddenly flooded with shame. She could do without his vote. He raised a hand and waved.

~

That afternoon he left a voice mail message at her office. "Whenever you want to get that steak," he said. "Just let me know. I want to hear more about this contract." He left another the following morning, and at lunch a bouquet of lilies appeared on her desk. She wanted to hide them before anyone noticed. The office thrived on gossip, and she'd never hear the end of it, how she had a new pet, how she'd do anything for her job. The flowers were gaudy but beautiful—orange petals spotted with black—and she couldn't bring herself to throw them away. She tore up the note and left the vase in the break room. When she returned from a meeting late in the afternoon, the lilies were back on her desk, with a handwritten cardboard sign: *Grand Old Prostitution.*

She was too busy to be bothered. The Budget Committee had already begun hearings on the union bill, and she was making her last pitch to members who hadn't yet committed. She told herself she was too busy to get back to Gearhart, too, though she found herself actively avoiding places where she'd likely run into him, the cafeteria, the Assembly lounge, the parking lot closest to the State House. She didn't answer the phone when she was in the office, pretending to be too absorbed in paperwork to break her concentration. Normally she spent time in the gallery, assessing the mood in the chamber, watching interactions among the members, but now she popped in only briefly, listening for half an hour to a debate about bilingual education. She sat in the back row, beside the door, hoping to keep Gearhart from spying her. He didn't take notes, didn't have the bill open in front of him. He played with his fingers, tugged at the sleeves of his jacket, shifted in his chair, craned his neck to see the people around him. When he did finally spot her, he gave a jovial smile and pointed a forefinger at her, thumb raised like a pistol's hammer. She pretended not to notice and after a moment slipped away.

Then, for the rest of the week, the Budget Committee hearings occupied her attention. Ham Wheeler ran them as if they were the Nuremberg Trials. He bullied the union reps who took the stand, the state hospital workers, the corrections officers, the teachers—everyone but the firefighters, whom he praised for their bravery and sacrifice. Ellie didn't testify this time, but she still cringed whenever he spoke, remembering her first week on the job, the sickened feeling that had stayed with her for months, the dry heaves in the toilet stall. It was hard to believe how far she'd come. Wheeler attacked the liberal underpinnings of the bill and at the same time pushed it forward, a sleight of hand she'd come to admire, as uncomfortable as it made her to watch. He'd make a good congressman, she thought, even if he stood against everything she believed in.

The soccer players had moved out of the motel, but she could hardly sleep. Three days in a row she'd caught Val just as she was heading down to the subway or into a meeting, and they weren't able to talk. Val's spirits sounded high, but with the hurried greetings and interference on their cell phones, it was hard to be sure. Ellie considered going home for the weekend to check in, but there was too much to get done. If she let up now, what was the point of all her effort?

Late Friday afternoon, as she was hurrying down the State House steps on her way to debrief her team on the committee hearing, a hand gripped her arm, just above the elbow. She recognized the slender fingers and bulging forearm before she looked up to see their owner. "Eleanor," Gearhart said, leaning away to look at her, as if trying to place her amid a swirl of hazy memories. "What a surprise."

"I'm afraid I can't talk now, Assemblyman. I'm running late."

"Maybe you tried to get in touch with me about dinner," he said. "I've been so busy I haven't checked my messages."

His hand was still on her arm, fingers making soft, caressing motions through her sleeve. Staffers and lobbyists hurried past them on either side. Bus brakes squealed on State Street. She didn't find him attractive, not at all. The men she'd gone for in her younger days had all been rugged and brooding, with dark eyes and delicate features. Gearhart's skin was flawless and scrubbed, no pores visible, not even a hint of stubble. He smiled without squinting, which gave his face a stricken, half-witted look. "You shouldn't send me flowers," Ellie said. "People will get the wrong impression."

"Things are finally quieting down for me," Gearhart said. "I'm free tonight, as a matter of fact."

"I don't think—"

"I can pick you up at seven-thirty," he said. "You're staying at the Red Roof Inn?"

"I can't make it this evening," Ellie said, trying to free her arm, gently, without success. His fingers managed to hold their grip, though they seemed hardly to apply any pressure, thumb still rubbing circles in the soft, vulnerable flesh between muscle and bone. She hoped to see someone she recognized, to catch an eye and appeal for help, but no one paid them any attention. "Really, I am running late," she said. "I'm going to have to leave now."

"I'll meet you in the lobby," he said, the stricken look exacerbated by what seemed to be reddening eyes, as if he were about to cry. "Wear something nice."

"You've got to stop," Ellie said, now actively trying to pry his fingers away. They caught somehow on her blouse, wound up in the fabric of her sleeve and hard to get loose. "I'll report you. I'll call the Ethics Committee."

"Off to an appointment now," he said. "See you at seven-thirty." He leaned forward, those slick lips pursed and coming toward hers. She didn't believe it at first, and by the time she did it was too late to turn away. Her own lips were suddenly moist and tingling. And then her arm was free, and Gearhart was hurrying past her down the steps. She didn't move. The State House pillars towered above her. A car horn blared. The mild wind brought exhaust, recalling the rotten, salty smell of the Waterway. An aide she recognized but whose name she couldn't remember said hello. She didn't know if he'd seen the kiss. She didn't answer.

It was astonishment she felt more than anger, and that strange cloudiness of vision and thought that had plagued her since her first sleepless night in Trenton. Anger was something she talked herself into as she finally gathered herself and made her way to Gearhart's office in the State House Annex. She was incensed by the time she made it to his door, marching past a bored receptionist, not stopping to announce herself. He was alone behind his empty desk. No appointment, no busy schedule. This office was barren, not at all like his suite in Forked River— no portraits on the wall, no texts on the bookshelves. He stood when she came in and pulled out a chair for her, but she didn't sit. She paced in front of his desk, and he flopped back into his chair. The window behind him looked out on the golden knob of the State House dome. "Are you out of your mind?" she said. "Do you want to get me fired?"

"I'm sorry," he said, holding his head in both hands, elbows on the desk. "I couldn't help myself."

"You'd better start helping yourself. I'm calling a lawyer."

"I don't know what you've done to me."

"I haven't done anything," she said. "And I'm not going to do anything."

"If we just got to know each other a little—"

"You're married, Assemblyman. You've got two kids, remember?"

He lifted his head, briefly, just long enough to show her a suffering look, and then let his face sink back into his hands. It amazed her to think she could have this effect on him, on anyone, after all this time. "She doesn't understand me," he said, without conviction, as if it were something he'd made up on the spot.

"I'm not interested in your family troubles," Ellie said, growing calmer now, sensing the power she had over him, how easily she could hurt him. It almost made her feel sorry for him. "I'm not interested in you. I'm queer, okay? I'm interested in women." He didn't answer. If he was surprised, or if the revelation offended his conservative sensibilities, he didn't let on. She finally sat in the chair he'd offered and lowered her voice. "Look, Jordan," she said, and took note of how his body shifted at the sound of his name, an almost imperceptible straightening of his shoulders, his head lifting a few degrees. He was just a kid, as Wheeler had said. He didn't know what he was doing. "I'm sorry you got the wrong impression," she went on. "Maybe I could have made myself clearer from the start…I thought I had, but if I made you think—"

"I read your bill," he said, raising his head again, smiling now, the wounded expression fading from those oddly plastic, shining features.

"And?"

"I don't know if I'll be able to vote for it."

"I didn't think you would."

"You know, my constituents—"

"You've got to vote your conscience."

"And I've gotten calls from a number of my colleagues…"

She waited a moment, watching him closely. Again she couldn't decide which was real, the confident arrogance or the fumbling boyishness. "Which colleagues?"

"There seems to be," he said, and glanced up at the ceiling, as if searching for the right word, "consensus. Among the leadership. They want to vote it down."

"I don't believe you. Who did you talk to?"

Gearhart shrugged, smiled, leaned back in his chair. "I didn't commit to anything. I told them I've got to think about it. I've got a mind of my own."

"If you heard from Wheeler, you'd know there's bi-partisan support," she said. "He's been on our side from the beginning."

"I can still be convinced," Gearhart said.

"I'm not going to dinner with you, Assemblyman."

"That's fine," he said. "We don't have to go to dinner."

"Then what do you want?"

He smiled wider, leaned back farther, crossed his legs, locked his hands behind his head. "Take a guess."

~

On Monday morning, she came into the office to find dour faces and mournful silence. There was news. Hadn't she heard? The bill was being pushed to the floor early, with only half an afternoon slated for debate. A vote could come as early as tomorrow morning. The newest numbers didn't look promising. They were almost out of time.

She hurried to Ham Wheeler's office. His assistant made her wait twenty minutes, though the session was set to open in half an hour. Ellie had known the assistant for four years now, had heard stories about her children and grandchildren, had sent her a get-well card after her hysterectomy. But today she might as well have been a stranger—the stout woman hardly acknowledged her, ignoring her short breath, her raised voice, saying with chilly politeness that Wheeler was on the phone and would be with her as soon as possible. Wouldn't she take a seat?

When she was finally let in, she had to stand for another minute as Wheeler pretended to study a memo on his desk, only slowly pulling his gaze away and propping his glasses on top of his head. "Miss Schatz," he said. "You don't look so hot. Trouble at home?"

Her tongue was dry, sticky. She tried to swallow but couldn't. "The vote," she said. "It's coming up tomorrow?"

"That's how it looks."

"But I thought we'd get two days of testimony. The whole chamber was supposed to hear what the committee heard. They don't know what they're voting on."

"I'm just one member," Wheeler said, raising both hands, palms up. Even though she knew it was phony, the gruff voice had its desired effect of making her weak-kneed. She couldn't help feeling that she was the one who'd done something wrong, the one guilty of betrayal. On his desk he had a smaller photo than the one in his district office, this showing Bogart staring furiously into Lauren Bacall's eyes, as if he wanted to slap her, or kiss her, or both. "I don't control everything."

"You're the committee chair."

"There's pressure from all sides. We've got three-dozen bills to consider this session. Yours isn't the only one."

"We don't have the numbers yet."

Wheeler sighed and pulled his glasses down onto his nose.

"You're not going to get the numbers. I've known that for two weeks already. You never made any headway in District 23, and you lost Somerset County."

"If we had more time—"

"Come on," he said. "It's not going to happen. No matter what you do. You've got to know when to throw in the towel."

No matter what she did. On Friday afternoon, she'd been too stunned to say anything as she left Gearhart's office, his words following her slow footsteps to the door. What got her most was how sad it made her, to think that his strange pursuit of her came down to nothing but this: a tawdry proposition, a sexual bribe. She knew why she'd been so tickled the first time she'd visited his office, laughing as she drove home. She'd pictured herself walking down the street with him, the two of them attracting the smiles of everyone who passed, such a good-looking couple, the least-threatening sight you could imagine. How long had she craved a life that was easier, that wasn't made up of one struggle after another? On her way across his office she wanted to cry, but she managed to keep her posture straight, her hand firm as she slammed his door behind her. Would she have done anything different if she'd known then what was coming?

"There's still tonight," she said to Wheeler now. "The ones on the fence. We can get them on board."

"Not me," Wheeler said. "I'm through."

"But," she said, and felt herself blinking, dry mouth seared by the air passing through. "But you're on my side."

"Sorry, kid," he said out of the corner of his mouth. "Can't ride a losing horse into Congress." He did a lousy Bogart impression, and anyway it wasn't a Bogart line—it belonged to one of the criminals in the books he and his siblings were named for, someone with no code of loyalty or allegiance. Her face must have betrayed her, even as she tried to hide the depth of her disappointment. Wheeler's expression softened, the kindly, caring look returning, a sorrowful, understanding half-smile. Her blinking quickened, and now she had to wipe at her eyes with the back of her hand. "Listen, Ellie," he said. "Sometimes it's okay to give up."

~

She told herself she wouldn't watch the vote, but she found herself in the gallery anyway, reading the digital scoreboard, listening as the clerk read out the numbers and the Speaker repeated them: 37 in the affirmative, 42 in the negative, 0 abstentions. Ham Wheeler looked satisfied, nodding to the assemblyman beside him, thumbs hooked in his belt. Jordan Gearhart's seat was empty. Ellie wasn't surprised. She'd gone straight to his office after leaving Wheeler's yesterday morning, but his door was locked, his secretary gone. What would she have done if he'd been there? Agreed to dinner? Given him her room key? Threatened to sue him unless he voted for the contract? She had too much integrity even for that, she thought, too much self-respect, and then tried but failed to feel proud of herself. His vote wouldn't have mattered, but still she couldn't keep a frustrating thought from nagging her: she hadn't done all she could. The Speaker called for the next vote, on a bill that would bar sex offenders from jobs that involved working with children. It passed without any challenge.

She left the gallery and the State House and spent an hour in her office, commiserating with her co-workers, with her boss who reassured her that she'd done her best. Then she was on the road, heading home. It was only mid-afternoon when she made it back to the apartment, but Val was there already, coming out of the bedroom as Ellie closed the door. The noise startled Val, and she gave a little yelp, nearly dropping the plant she was carrying, an orchid her brother had given her when she and Ellie had first moved in together. "You're back," Val said, frozen in the bedroom doorway.

"You're not at work," Ellie said.

"I took a personal day."

"Good for you." She dropped her suitcase and slipped off her shoes. She was too tired to look for signs of Val's depression, to gauge if she were on the verge of another breakdown. For once she wanted Val to take care of herself. She dropped onto the sofa, but Val didn't join her, didn't move from where she stood. The orchid had had enormous white blossoms when they'd first gotten it, but it had never bloomed again, not even after they remembered to fertilize it. It just kept sending out sinewy roots over the rim of the pot, its leaves growing longer, drooping. Ellie had wanted to get rid of it a dozen times, but Val would never let her. Maybe now she was finally ready. "We didn't get the votes, if you want to know."

Val was in her yoga clothes, gray stretch pants that didn't fit her anymore, a loose cotton wrap that tied at the waist, black backless clogs. Ellie couldn't remember the last time she'd looked so comfortable. "I found a place. West 73rd. Two stops from Whole Foods."

"We lost," Ellie said.

"Right around the corner from Riverside Park. A block from Broadway."

"All that work, for nothing."

"I already took it," Val said. "I signed the lease Friday."

Ellie sat up. Out the window the lights of Midtown stretched halfway across the placid river. Her father had always called Manhattan a floating toilet, a repository for all the shit in the world. "You what?"

"I knew you wouldn't want to," Val said. "That's why I did it myself."

"And you just expect me to pick up and go?"

"No," Val said, staring down at the orchid, the roots draped over her fingers like tentacles. "I expect you to stay."

It was only then that Ellie noticed the changes. Prints missing from the walls, the coffee table empty of vases, the bookshelves half-cleared, the remaining books toppled onto their sides. And there was a change in Val, too. How could it have taken this long to notice? She'd gotten a haircut, a stylish crop above her ears that made her look five years younger, the gray speckles dyed back to brown. Her chin was puckered, her forehead creased. Ellie hadn't seen this expression on Val's face—sympathetic, unselfish—since the weeks after her father's funeral. And it was this more than anything that set Ellie crying now, protesting, saying how unfair it was for Val to leave her, how cruel. Val only shook her head. They wanted different things, she said. There was no reason to torture themselves or each other forever.

"We can work something out," Ellie said, and immediately felt pitiful, as she had when she'd cried in Ham Wheeler's office.

"We've worked out enough already," Val said, and set the plant down at her feet, its meaty leaves bending upward. What an awful, ugly thing right there in the middle of the floor, where Ellie couldn't ignore it.

"This is completely out of the blue."

"Oh, Ellie," Val said. "Don't do this. We've both known it was coming for a long time."

She argued for most of the afternoon and evening, but she knew Val was right. This was as predictable as everything else in their relationship. First there'd been the sudden, blissful tumble into love, and for the past two years the slow, excruciating climb out of it. It was curious to feel both devastated and relieved at the same time. How could something be at once what she wanted and the worst thing in the world? At some point in the night, she and Val went from crying to laughing and back. Then Val took her to bed. And here was one thing that hadn't changed—that leap off the cliff, that shuddering descent, that breathless landing. She slept, unmoving, untroubled, for the first time in a week.

~

In the morning, Val took away the orchid and the last of her clothes. Ellie was famished. All she found in the fridge was a tub of olives from Whole Foods, and she ate them standing at the window, spitting pits onto the floor. Fog hovered over the river, a massive luxury liner pulling into the 52nd Street pier. Somewhere off to the right, blocked by expensive condos, was the gaping hole in the skyline that had rattled her father, that reminded him, he'd said the last time she'd seen him alive, to expect everything he built to eventually fall apart.

That was three weeks before he died, at the Passover seder her mother had begged Ellie and Val to come to, refusing to listen when Ellie made excuses. He was mostly cheerful that night, joking all the way through the prayers and the four glasses of wine and the ritual marking of the ten plagues. "Hemorrhoids," he said, dipping his pinkie into his glass and touching it to the edge of his plate. "Athlete's foot. Syphilis." The flimsy yamulka perched on top of his head like an umbrella missing its handle. During dinner Val talked basketball with him, while Ellie argued politics with her older sister, a married health administrator with two overweight kids.

A normal life. After all this time. That's what Ellie thought until the end of the night, when they were about to leave. As they stood in the foyer, her mother retrieving their jackets from the closet, Val, just briefly, slipped her arm around Ellie's waist. Her father flinched. No one else noticed, as far as Ellie knew, and she doubted her father realized she'd seen.

But she had—a cloud of disgust passed over his features and left in its wake a squinting, impatient expression that lingered as they said their goodbyes. He hugged Ellie half-heartedly, hands patting her hips, and quickly let her go. She cried the whole way home, inconsolable, and it was Val who was outraged, cursing him as she drove. A father's love wasn't supposed to be conditional, she said. It was supposed to be something you could count on. But Ellie had known for years by then that that was only partly true.

Was he happy now? Would he finally leave her alone?

She turned away from the window. It didn't do any good to negotiate with the dead. She couldn't please her father now any more than she could punish him. She couldn't love him any more than she had, or hate him more. All she could do was miss him, and that was growing harder with every passing day.

It was enough to deal with the living. The union would

regroup. They'd draft a new bill, a temporary contract that would keep their workers from striking. She'd call Ham Wheeler, assure him there were no hard feelings, get him to pledge his support for the revised contract. She'd start driving the state, from the Water Gap to the Pine Barrens, up and down the shore.

In a month she'd be back in traffic on the Parkway, which she'd first ridden with her father at eight years old, a day of hooky from work and school, too cold for sitting on the beach, but nice enough for walking, for visiting lighthouses, for playing games on the boardwalk. They crept along with trucks and busloads of seniors heading to Atlantic City, ticking off exit numbers, reading out the names of towns she'd now come to know so well: Keyport, Holmdel, Red Bank, Eatontown, Allenwood, Brick, Beachwood, Lacey, Forked River. She complained the whole way, asking why it was taking so long, pretending to get carsick, and her father ignored her, fiddling with the radio that picked up mostly static, shouting at drivers who cut him off. Finally, he put on his turn signal and handed her a quarter. She leaned across him, tossed the coin into the basket of the automated tollbooth and watched, amazed, as the gate opened to let them through.

Abby E. Murray

Small Evil Bone

My father, exhausted from pneumonia
and sailing further out on the sea
inside his lungs, asks if he's told me
about his deer problem. They're eating
his roses. He had a nice big yellow one
that disappeared yesterday morning,
now he's got a garden full of bite marks.
I am visiting from my ninth-story condo
and I would love to see a deer snuffle
through dirt still packed where my knees
had once been, to kneel in dirt at all,
to know the beast hardly tugged the petals
off the buds before they melted
on its sandpaper tongue and not once
did it think, *these are not my roses.*

My father has a hunting rifle in the closet
standing up behind the Christmas wrapping
paper and I'm afraid he will remember.
He's started naming his roses after us.
But he says he's just been sitting outside
under the hanging fuschias, the air is good
for him there, and when he sees them coming,
there's three, a doe and two babes,
he yells SHOO! and it seems to do the trick.
They go bounding off, he says, into
the gravel pit across the road. Most of me
is relieved to hear it—all but the small evil bone
I have banished to the pit of my spine,
a splinter of a bone, a chip, the one
that recalls so quickly where the gun is.

Abby E. Murray

FREE MARKETS

There's competition on our street between ice cream vendors.
I don't buy, just sit on the porch at night nursing my Guinness,
count the school kids sorting coins in their hands as they run.
I'm rooting for the only vendor who doesn't drive a van,
who pushes a metal cart up the hill with bells tied to it,
bells of all shapes and sizes, clumps of Christmas bells
and cowbells that clang with his step, slowly chipping away
the white clouds painted on his steel cooler. When I see the vans
drag by each other, leaking radiator fluid and a squashed version
of *Small World* what I really think about is when are the lot of them
going to duke it out and fight for our neighborhood purse?
When's the ice cream war going to start and God I hope I'm there
to see it, lined up on the sidewalk with the kids when fudgesicles
and nutty-buddies shoot down the street like arrows, scoops of vanilla
chocolate swirl catapulted from half-moon spoons, all of them
aimed at speakers or windows or decals. That's when
the man with the cart is going to shine—you watch—
my speakerless, windowless, two-wheeled-cooler sweetsie vendor,
armed for the fight with nothing to lose but a couple of silver bells
stuffed up an exhaust pipe while the battle's in full swing.

North Carolina

I realized some time back that our existence on this earth leaves a mark. I tried, for a while, to close my eyes and envision a landscape 150 years in the past. Eventually, through much pain and discomfort, I understood that the change our human presence leaves behind is not going anywhere. It was then that I began to experience our relationship with this land in a different light; it was then that I began to see beauty in the darkness. Signposts rise from the asphalt parking lots to form the church steeples of our day, while the oil derricks arrange themselves on the horizon like sculptures on Easter Island. These scenes in our everyday world speak of the needs, desires, and ambitions of our day and point to where we may be tomorrow. And though I have managed to find an appreciation for our man-altered world, I have not been left blind to it's consequences. Through my work I attempt to explore the complexity of our role within our environment.

-Shane Darwent

Michael Delp

THERAPY

We'd been out road-hunting. Cofer drove and I watched for partridge in the trees. When we saw any, we'd pull the truck over about a hundred yards from where we spotted them and then sneak up through the woods and open fire.

Maybe that's what got Cofer going, driving for an hour without seeing a single bird, but from the way he looked when he picked me up I could tell something was wrong. His face had the look of a guy who had been crawling along a high ledge for hours. He looked white and exhausted. "Bleak," he said when I asked him how he was when I got in, and bleak he stayed.

I tried all sorts of things to cheer him up. I told the same farting jokes I always told when we rode in the truck. I knew Marlene had been on him the whole week about getting a job again. Last weekend she made him drive all the way to town for a box of Ding Dongs. The only reason I know is that I'm Cofer's only friend and so when he goes, I go. Whether it's Ding Dongs or Kotex, I get the nod. Shotgun is where I ride.

And what drives Cofer nuts most is fiddling with the radio dial. So, last weekend, on the Ding Dong trip I fiddled like crazy: up and down, over and over. He hated it when I did it too fast. "Christ," he'd say. "Move it slow, don't tax nothing."

That was Cofer's whole philosophy of life: don't tax nothing. Take everything slow. Real slow. But I fiddled anyway, short bursts of country western tunes, then I'd switch to that classical station both of us hated. He'd swerve the truck and say, every time, "You dickhead," then switch it back to the station that played only oldies.

I suspected he was out of sorts when he picked me up today for the pat patrol, which is the name he gave it, not me. When he said it, "pat patrol," he made a sound like a little kid playing with a toy police car, his finger whirling in the air.

The radio was off when I got in and he was sort of half humming something by the Righteous Brothers. When I asked him something about not having the radio on after he said he was so bleak, all he could do was drop into low gear and take off. "I'm telling you, this time, I'm really telling you," he muttered, the truck inching out of my driveway.

After several miles of listening to him hum, I couldn't stand it any longer. "It's Marlene again, ain't it?" I said.

And he said, almost as if a ghost was talking, "Yeah."

"What's wrong now?" I asked.

"Her mother's coming to live with us next week for good. And I'm leaving. Just told her today. Check the bed," he said, pointing with his thumb behind the cab.

When I looked through the window all I could see was piles of clothes shifting in the wind, some old Playboys flapping around, an 8-track stereo and a pair of waders. Just like it looked the last time he threatened to move out, only this time he said he was serious.

"No kidding," I said, playing along.

"No shit, Dick Tracy," he mumbled back. Then I saw them through the flecks of snow on the windshield, a whole maple tree full of partridge sitting like ornaments on a Christmas tree. I motioned toward the sky and Cofer slowed down, looked up through the window and it was then I could see he was crying.

When he knew that I knew, he looked directly at me and started shaking. "You gotta help me," he said. He knew, because I was truly his only friend; because I had a sense that he sensed I had known for months that he was inching along that narrow ledge of our lives when the first and last impulse is to just let yourself go; he knew I would have to help. I was bound to help no matter how stupid or ill-conceived the ideas was. Even if it was dangerous, Cofer knew I'd be there.

"Pull off," I said. And Cofer aimed the truck over toward the shoulder, reaching under the seat as he slid out. "Don't forget your gun," I said.

"Don't need it," he whispered back, opening the hood of the truck.

He had a set of jumper cables in his hand. When I got out and stood next to him, he started to hook them up, positive to positive, negative to negative. "Remember," he said, "You're helping," motioning me closer. When I got next to him I could see how red his eyes really were, the pupils dark and tiny like to knobs to cheap hotel door rooms where strangers slept in the cold.

In half a voice he told me to hold the negative clamp while he hooked the positive cable to his left ear, no sign in his face of pain, only pure vacancy.

"What in the fuck are you doing?" I shouted.

"Just help!" he shouted back.

"But Christ, Cofer, It can't be bad enough to kill yourself," I said.

"Nobody's dying, now help," he said, forcing the negative clamp into my hand, motioning for me to touch the positive clamp to his leg.

I waited for a second or two for the joke to show itself, the way it always did when he was up to something stupid. He had done something like this before: once with his hat full of lighter fluid at the Hofbrau bar, he had threatened, in despair again, to light it on fire and put it on. Only then, he lit the match, and just before he dropped it into the hat, he put the flame inside his mouth and snuffed it out with his breath, laughing until he fell off his chair.

I shook him just once.

"Do it," he said. "This ain't like that hat trick at the bar."

"Jesus, you are serious," I said noticing now, some kind of odd resolve that had seemed to reshape the bones of his face. He looked quiet, still, like some bird of prey about to drop down on a piece of road-kill.

He reached for my hand and slid it up his pant leg, the other clamp pinching the grey-white skin of his calf. Then he stood upright and took off his glove, touching his wedding band to the battery terminal. A blue arc lifted, almost in slow motion from the battery, traveled up his left arm and then his whole body shook, only for a second or two. He fell back into the snow and I stood above him, just staring at him.

Then I started laughing, laughing as hard as I ever had, then he started half moaning half laughing and I could hear that old laugh of his, the one that starts deep in the pit of the stomach, that place you fall into every day if you're really crazy and then he sat up and laughed harder than me.

"Just needed that to straighten me out," he said. "I figured that one out the other night when Marlene was watching one of them old horror movies, you know, the lightning coming into a dark operating room straight into the monster's head."

I helped him up and brushed him off, noticing how he looked like he had just been brought back to life, like some cartoon character who had just fallen off a cliff and hit bottom, only to get back up and miraculously resume the chase.

I wanted to hold him, maybe shake him up a bit out of relief, or anger, I didn't know which. But I didn't. Friends like we are don't do that kind of thing. A friend just goes with you on something, wherever you're going, or does whatever you're doing. No comment is needed to hold up their end.

And that's what it was all the way home, no comment about the cables. We stopped at the Hofbrau for a six to go, then cracked one open for each of us, both of us staring up at the darkening sky, a few stars just beginning to show. I wanted to speak, but we stayed silent, drinking our first beer there in the gravel lot of the bar, then jumped back in and jammed up the radio.

On the way back home I could still smell the odor of electricity in the cab. A smell I thought seemed like what burnt stars must smell like. Cofer was still laughing, drinking a last road beer. Before he dropped me off we swung toward his house and Cofer shut of his lights while we drifted past his picture window. Marlene was lifting the baby up into the air, then bringing her down gently against her knee. I could hear Cofer weakening and when Marlene stood up and walked toward the Christmas tree holding his daughter's hand, I knew he'd cave in.

After he dropped me off in my driveway, I knew he'd go back home like he always does and sit up half the night in the living room. Marlene would be asleep on the couch, the baby tight under her arms and Cofer would be cleaning his rifle. I knew from what he'd told me before that his mind would be fluttering like a confusion of birds lifting off in a forest. He'd get the urge to just drive, leave in the middle of the night and drive until he collapsed. But he always stayed home and I knew he'd stand over the baby's bed for ten or fifteen minutes that night, watching her chest lift up and down like there were delicate wings inside of her.

When I went to bed all I could smell was that blue arc lifting him off the ground, and I fell asleep to the memory of the sound of his jumper cables dangling over the tailgate, bouncing and hitting the freshly plowed blacktop, then striking against the back of his truck, the rhythm of tiny sparks as they clicked together spitting into the night.

Watching the Takeoff—Helena, GA

Alvin—Aiken, SC

Shannon Huffman Polson

Inheriting An Alaskan Log Cabin

We should have known that first visit back to the cabin in Alaska would be different. I had been coming for fifteen years to my family cabin, but my husband Peter had been only once before, on a snowy Thanksgiving several years prior. To return to a place we had been before only as guests—but this time as owners, as inheritors of a place after my father and stepmother died—could never be the same. Now we were responsible. Now our visit carried the weight of attention.

It was fall. Sun sifted through yellow aspen and dark green spruce, spattering the gravel driveway leading directly off of the two lane Parks Highway. We drove down the driveway with eyes wide and scared as new parents, as if adopting a child with no notice, not knowing the first thing about how to take care of it. How do you earn ownership? How do you deserve inheritance?

Walking onto the deck of the small cabin, we looked down the bluff to the river below. The mountains beyond spread like soft folds of fabric, blues and greens painted with swaths of gold. Just past the cabin sat the outhouse, also on the bluff, a wide window on the front wall looking out to the river. A propane tank and an oil tank sat outside of the cabin. We put the key in the lock of the heavy door. It needed a firm push to open. We walked inside.

The well-trod plywood floors creaked underfoot. The smell of dust hung in the air, rising from the forty-year-old gold carpet in the living room. Narrow stairs, also carpeted, led from the kitchen to two upstairs bedrooms. The spruce log walls stood out as the primary feature, a warm amber hue from years of mellowing. Propane lights hung on the walls, remnants of the cabin's earlier years without electricity. Electric lights were sparse.

The view through wide windows showed the river curving west and then east, making its way north.

We didn't have to be experts to understand that, as much as the logs from which they are made, cabins are structures of stories supporting memory and possibility, past and future. We had heard the stories over the years: how the original owners of the cabin cut the logs and pulled them by dogsled, three at a time. How they let them dry for a year, and then peeled them by hand. How when cabin dwellers visited each other in the winter months, the knock on the front door was called "the call of the wild." Some of these stories proved true; some, I found later, were an intricate blend of myth and history.

We didn't have to be experts to understand that, as much as the logs from which they are made, cabins are structures of stories supporting memory and possibility, past and future. We had heard the stories over the years: how the original owners of the cabin cut the logs and pulled them by dogsled, three at a time. How they let them dry for a year, and then peeled them by hand. How when cabin dwellers visited each other in the winter months, the knock on the front door was called "the call of the wild." Some of these stories proved true; some, I found later, were an intricate blend of myth and history.

Any place requires care and Peter, and I needed to learn to be stewards. Advice trickled in: burn the wood stove hot to rid the chimney of creosote before letting it burn slow, since chimney fires are the biggest cause of cabins burning; put sugar-water (a natural anti-freeze) down the drains before leaving the cabin in the winter to keep the U-joints clear.

Without the stories, the history, and knowledge of maintaining a log cabin, we didn't know where to begin. It seemed to make sense that we start by talking to the old-timers. These were people who were part of the history holding up the cabin. This was an adoption, after all, and not a birth.

~

It was the end of the week when we visited with Bill and Ree. It was Bill's eighty-ninth birthday. He wore a plaid wool shirt and suspenders, and was stouter than earlier years. Blind for twenty years, Bill's resourcefulness was legendary. After losing his sight, he plumbed his own cabin by feel, using a file to mark the length of the pipes he measured so that he could read where to cut them like Braille. Bill loved opera, mostly the Italian ones, and read investment books using a large reading contraption sitting on the kitchen table.

Ree was a quilter of international renown, an art form she came to after developing an allergy to the materials she used for silk-screening. Bill and Ree raised two sons in their cabin sitting on the edge of the tiny Deneki Lake. Until recently, their cabin was dry, the term used for cabins without running water. Over the long winters, Ree melted snow for water for all of her household tasks, including washing cloth diapers.

Bill sat on an ancient gold couch facing a large picture window. My husband and I sat opposite him on handcrafted rocking chairs, and Ree glanced at us from the kitchen.

"Our neighbors say you're the one who taught them how to build a cabin," I said to Bill. "How did you figure it out?"

My speech felt awkward, halting with guilt that I was asking for stories we hadn't yet earned, stories that would come naturally if we were residents, if we'd put in our time and had something to offer in return. We had nothing to offer yet, no knowledge, no skills, and precious few stories. Bill didn't seem to mind.

"I guess I just got a book," he said, a mischievous smile on the corners of his mouth crinkling his eyes. "I think it was called *Building the Alaska Log Home*. Just a small book."

"Paperback," Ree added.

"That's right, just a small paperback book," Bill said, nodding slowly. His watery eyes looked toward the light from the window opening out to the lake and Carlo Mountain beyond. "I helped out the chief ranger with his cabin in Cantwell after that. Guess I just learned from reading and doing."

So that's all there was to it. We just had to figure it out. We would learn it, slowly, the way you learn about a person, conversation by conversation, experience by experience. I felt desperate to earn our place there, to anticipate needs, to put in work, to bind our lives to the cabin. So we started with the stories, letting them sink into us.

~

On our trip to the cabin the next fall, I noticed the logs looked a little bit weathered, the stain on the deck worn thin. Fall had always been my favorite time at the cabin with my family, and I easily convinced my husband to make our annual visits at the end of August and early September when we could pick berries in the crisp air and watch the tundra turn red. It was still early enough in the season to get work done, too. When not at the cabin, we lived in Seattle where we hired specialists, people who did roofs or gutters, landscaping or electrical work. In remote areas, everyone was a generalist, because they had to be. In *Building the Alaska Log Home*, Tom Walker warns that, "There isn't any substitute for hard work, sweat and patience." To live in this cabin required that our sweat mingle with the life of the logs and their history.

One of the best things about our log cabin was the very thing that put it at risk. It was an organic structure, subject to the same process of decay as all things organic. We had to work with the logs to protect what we loved about them, that they were made of the forest around us, from the very things we treasured. I suggested log oiling to my husband, tentatively, because I had no other ideas.

Doing our best to ignore feelings of inadequacy, we lay old bed sheets and newspaper on the deck. Peter used blue painter's tape to cover the windows. We dipped brushes into a can of log oil, letting oil soak into the bristles, saturating the bush. Then we took our brushes and began stroking the logs. The bristles distributed the oil with each pass. The logs on the cabin's weathered north side gulped the layer of oil thirstily. We applied another layer. My shoulder and back muscles started to ache. I saw the logs as if for the first time, the grain of the wood, the places winter storms had been most cruel. This work required attention, not just to the labor, but to the cabin, to this thing that held our lives.

Somewhere we transitioned; we turned a corner we didn't even see. This was our cabin now. I smiled to myself as Peter looked over our notes. We thought we were adopting the cabin, but perhaps it had adopted us. There was no earning ownership, or deserving inheritance. There was only acceptance of the gift. I ran my hand slowly over one of the logs. It was rough and strong and beautiful. It held up the cabin as it was, and as it will be.

It was a few years later that the kitchen got to me. Peter and I bumped into each other one too many times in the dark corridor, the lamp on the rickety refrigerator and the propane light on the wall both inadequate to the task. I was annoyed that washing dishes required a headlamp. We didn't have the skills to do the overhaul required, but a neighbor who worked in Denali National Park and Preserve did. He was another old-timer. How did they all figure out how to do things? He laughed, looking at the floor. "None of us knew a damn thing!" he said. "Hell, the guy who built your cabin didn't know one thing about it. He got a book at the library and read it. I think he has two left thumbs and one's crooked, but your place has held up great." This time, his story comforted me. Even the people learning as they went made it work.

Sketching out plans with pen and paper, we considered how the family we hoped to have would use the space, what we would want to include, how it would be crafted. As we talked, it occurred to me that we were doing new things. We were making new decisions. We were, as Bill had explained to us, figuring it out. Somewhere we transitioned; we turned a corner we didn't even see. This was our cabin now. I smiled to myself as Peter looked over our notes. We thought we were adopting the cabin, but perhaps it had adopted us. There was no earning ownership, or deserving inheritance. There was only acceptance of the gift. I ran my hand slowly over one of the logs. It was rough and strong and beautiful. It held up the cabin as it was, and as it will be.

~

It is an early March evening, and Peter and I are reading to the sonorous music of Johnny Cash, our newly assigned soundtrack for the cabin. I am lying on the couch, my eyelids falling with the darkness. Heat from the wood stove nestles into the fleece blanket covering me as the scene outside fades into reflections of lamplight on windows.

Peter's voice breaks through my reverie.

"Shannon, did you hear that?" He appears suddenly around the corner of the wall separating the dining and living rooms.

"What?" I ask, squinting against sleep.

"Owls! The Great Horned Owls!" I sit straight up, all vestiges of relaxation gone.

This is the time, early March, when we hear them along the bluff, calling for mates, their deep "Whoo's" called and answered in the darkness. We hear them most frequently on trips to the outhouse, inviting us to the mystery of their world, a world surrounding us even if we cannot always see it. "You can always hear them," a neighbor once told us, "but you won't find them."

We put on our boots, parkas and hats, grabbing flashlights as we run out of the cabin into the moonless snowy night. The abrupt transition from the warmth of the cabin to this frozen world slashes at my face and neck. In the below-zero temperatures, snow squeaks under our boots. Silhouettes of spruce take shape as our eyes adjust to the dark.

We are moving too fast; the sound of boots and panting take over. We stop and stand still, listening. The owl is just in front of us now. "Whoo, whooooo," comes the call. Farther down the bluff another answers it, the call riding the breath of wind through twisted branches of spruce and graceful lines of leafless aspen. Peter shines the flashlight to the top of the tree in front of us. Only scraggly branches show. We take another few steps forward, and the white beam of light slices through the dark, leaping to the top of another tree.

I see the owl. It is an extension of the tree's form, black on blackness, telltale ears pointing straight up. The owl's head swivels, and enormous eyes glare down on us, round and bright. Its body seems too big, unwieldy, impossible for the tree to support. Then it makes another, different sound—a raucous screech like a needle pulled across a record. It is a creature of and in the night, of and in the wild. I am speechless, and I am scared. I inhale, and the winter air stops at the back of my mouth.

We are intruding, inviting ourselves to bumble out of our cabin into this wild space. I stare, grateful and embarrassed, and turn back to the cabin hoping for forgiveness. Peter lingers. "Did you see its wingspan?" he asks. I didn't—I turned in the dark too soon, just before the owl lifted its body on wide wings as easily as if it were made of air. Peter was right to linger. This is part of our education, too. We shut ourselves in and away from our world at peril of our lives. Understanding this connection to life outside, how we are part of this mystery even in observation, might change life as we know it. Understanding this connection is grace itself.

More slowly than we left the cabin, we make our way back. The glow from the window is yellow as a flame. We enter back through the heavy door, bringing a little bit of wildness inside with us.

Nathan Graziano

IN ANTICIPATION OF MY NEXT BAD DECISION

Saturday afternoon sits like a bully on my head.
I crack another beer and watch college football,
those impossibly beautiful cheerleaders smiling

on the sidelines in those impossibly short skirts.
They're launched like bright thoughts in the sky
with sturdy young men ready to catch them,

then they'll all crowd around the camera and wag
their index fingers—they're all Number One—
with Saturday night and nice lives ahead of them.

My therapist says I have a drinking problem
and calls it a form of insanity. He compares it
to a helium balloon I expect to stay grounded

without a string tying it to anything solid. He says
I should try to get some exercise in the winter
when I tend to get depressed, so tonight

I'm going to shadow box in the garage
by the light of a lamp my wife and I never used.
We bought it at a yard sale when we were broke

and eating pancakes for all three meals.
But I always had money for drinks, and I think
my therapist may have a point. It's something

I knew when I was in college and trying to plan
my next step up the stairs, but I'd stumble back down,
hitting the ground, with nobody there to catch me.

Abandoned Theme Park—La Junta, CO

Elspeth—Cherokee, KS

Brian Maxwell

THE RIGHT KIND OF LIGHT

He moved one town up the beach and became Russell again, leaving behind anything he couldn't fit in the trunk of his car. He was twenty-two, and he'd decided he wouldn't answer to "Snickers" anymore, even if it had been his father's name before he left. Here, Russell had been promised a job on the roofs, and he jumped at the chance to start over. So he loaded his Ford Maverick and headed up the line. There were plenty of towns on the Florida coast—at least he could live where people called him by his own name.

Finding a place proved easy, though he was closer to the pool halls and strip joints than he would have liked. Downtown was right up against the ocean. If he wanted to hear the waves, he had to listen to street life as well. The apartment had a single room and a cramped kitchen, and he used the back door so he didn't have to see the neighbors. He scored two chairs from a dumpster and a mattress from the *Shop of Gulls*, where the church ladies sold second hand goods. He knew they prayed for the folks in the beer bars because they told him as much every time he came in.

The job didn't last long. The crew boss had been a surf rep and a contest rider once, he'd even ridden with Russell's father, back when both men were young enough to stay in the scene. But now Jed Dickerson was all boss, and he had a habit of holding pay. Russell walked on the third week, sold his car for rent and waited. He knew the game was to try and collect, but the thought turned him black. Instead, he walked the beach at night, slept late. He hauled a card table in from the trash and set up an old Panasonic radio that had also been his father's. It picked up AM stations so he listened to the news. That was how he'd heard about the tropical storm: it was still closer to Africa than the Caribbean, but the forecasts suggested that they were in for a big one if the weather system held.

The window was open to catch the breeze and he could hear the sounds of downtown. He smoked out of boredom, stubbing the butts in a coffee cup. There were three surfboards lined up against the wall, all destined for the pawn shop if he couldn't score. He concentrated on the largest, the one he shaped himself for riding big waves. It had taken him an entire summer to form the blank just so and add a layer of fiberglass. When that had dried, he sanded until his fingers wore out, painted it red, put another layer of glass over the first. He could still make out his initials, carved into the foam underneath and, despite the imperfections, he felt proud to have built something that he could touch.

Upstairs, the neighbors were yelling. It was Friday night, and he knew that, back home, his sister would be getting ready for work, scurrying to find a sitter. Leaving her was hard—but he'd had enough of the boyfriends, and living under her roof hurt in a way he couldn't describe. She'd given him a bottle of Old Crow, though he didn't know how to drink whiskey. "You're moving to a *shit town*," she said. "A tourist trap." He thought of this now as he ran his hand across the crease in the label, wondering whether liquor could go sour, whether he'd know the difference anyway. Then he stood and stretched, gave the surfboard a last glance. If the storm did hit, that would be the stick to ride. He promised himself he'd fix it in the morning, repair the dings and straighten the loose fin. But now it was the weekend, and he figured the old boss was loose on the town. He might as well try to shake him for that roof money one last time.

Outside, the air felt humid even for July, and he thought about the storm as people milled around him, jostling for position on the narrow sidewalks. Rock music pumped out of the bars and the crowds were lively. He passed a few places that he deemed too bright and walked in the direction of the pier, looking for the kind of bar that might lead him to Jed Dickerson.

While he walked he tried to imagine a town on the coast of Africa, what it would look like, whether the streets would be busy.

The storm would have started there, a few hundred miles out to sea, no more menacing than a cluster of heavy clouds shaped like crumpled paper. But if it moved onward without breaking up, then great changes could begin to take place. His father used to talk about how storms began as seedlings, funnels of moisture far away. How the summer water heated with the sun and the rate of evaporation drove huge amounts of vapor upward where it gathered strength. That was how Russell's father imagined a storm: a mass of whirling summer heat pushed across the ocean's surface, feeding on the warm air, plodding slowly in whatever direction the trade winds pulled.

Russell compared the odds to the dream. For a storm to reach the Florida coast with waves as big as buildings, many things had to line up along the way. And because of this, when people begin to clamor at the possibility of rogue waves, sloped walls of water and surfing perfection, Russell knew that unless the system made it across the Atlantic full force, until it assumed the power to threaten Haiti or Cuba or one of the Keys, the storm would never even be given a name.

The Adirondack was a brick bar without windows and Russell had been inside only once before. The crowd had thinned out on the trek and he walked through the swinging doors, despite the motorcycles parked outside. Many of the pier bars were biker hangouts, dark places with concrete floors, but Dickerson was a bully, the sort who preferred the low murmur of drunks to the rowdiness of the strip.

It was quiet inside; a few roughnecks played pool in the background. Guitar riffs poured through the jukebox and he ordered a bottle of beer. The woman behind the counter didn't even look at his face and he took a seat along the wall. There were black and white photos nailed into the wood paneling, featuring surfers on long wooden boards. Behind them the ocean appeared tame, blue-green and almost transparent, as if all that water were merely a figment of the imagination. He sipped the beer. The room smelled of smoke and the televisions showed car races.

TRACHODON

No one watched. The few patrons seemed content amongst themselves; this was a neighborhood bar for people without neighborhoods to call their own.

A few younger guys came in, a pack of three in ripped Levi's and bright shirts with a mess of buttons down the front. Their hair was blond but they didn't appear to be surfers. The bigger of them had his hat turned sideways and he looked around as if he were sizing up the place. He said something and they all laughed, grabbed a few beers and began to circle the room. They weren't unlike the boys he'd grown up with, who spent too much money now on clothes and preferred fast cars with plastic spoilers along the rear. None of them surfed anymore; they messed around with pills instead, went to clubs, drove around all night until the sun came up and then went home to sleep. One of the bikers was gesturing across the bar and the three boys mocked him, staying close together even as they moved. The music throbbed and Russell could hear them shouting but not what they said. Jed Dickerson was nowhere to be seen, so he tipped his bottle and moved for the door.

The wind had picked up and the ocean gave off a fishy smell, the smell of low tide. He walked by the pier and circled back, slowing to count the lamps along the edges, the lights of the fisherman who stayed out all night tossing their nets into the shallows, trolling for tuna or mackerel or small sharks. He could see the red dots of their cigarettes. But the quiet was imposing; the world was asleep here. The tiny waves lapped the beach and the wind blew bits of trash across the sand. Russell put his hands in his pockets and walked back the way he'd come.

The houses were all one story and made of cinderblock, with sandy front yards and rusted mailboxes. The cars in the drives were rusty as well, and there were piles of dog shit every so often along the curbs. He'd expected something different. As silly as it sounded, he didn't think that here he'd have to stay up on the roofs, or work a lawn crew to earn a paycheck. But his sister was right: the only difference seemed to be that in this town there were more tourists, come for the palm trees and the long, white beaches, for the strip clubs and the shuttle launch. And they'd drink too much and crawl back to their ocean front hotels and before they left town in their rental cars, they'd make sure to search for the neighborhood where television crews had once filmed episodes of "I Dream of Jeannie."

The walk back seemed longer, and Russell saw the dull glow of neon spreading upward in the darkness before he heard the voices of the crowd. He walked through an alley and hesitated, watching the rush. Girls swam through the streets in short dresses, their tan shoulders sinewy and strong. The men were a mix of teens and old-timers, some bearded and stumbling, their boots and ratty jeans giving them away as laborers. The younger bunch looked much like the boys at the Adirondack: tall and packed with muscle, adorned in ball caps and unnecessarily white sneakers, as if everything rested on them distinguishing themselves from the drabness of the strip.

It was almost midnight and he made for a place just off the main drag, a wide-open bar without TVs or pictures on the wall. There wasn't even a sign: just a patch of glue drawn out in a line that once held a wooden bust that said Al's Lounge. There were no windows either and no neon lights. But Jed Dickerson haunted this place on work days; Russell had noticed more than once a cluster of work vans and roofing trailers parked in the dirt lot outside.

Now the place was mostly empty. An old blues number played in the background but the sound was muted, as if the speakers were blown or turned low. He ordered a bottle of Bud, took a stool. He shared the bar with two older guys, neither of which said hello or nodded when he sat down. They wore shorts and unlaced sneakers, no socks, and had thick calves and leathery necks.

They looked like old surfers. One of them poked at a pack of no name smokes, pushed it across the bar as if he were waiting to light up. The ashtray was full and Russell noticed their beards and the deep creases around their blue eyes. If his father hadn't taken his act to California, he might have ended up here, just like this, and he couldn't help but wonder if these men had sons on the strip somewhere, boys dealing dope or selling pills, wearing ball caps twisted to the side.

He drank quickly, ordered another as his companions nursed glasses of tap beer and sat in silence. He wondered about the storm again, what these men might do with the news if they snapped on the radio and heard about a tropical depression headed straight for the coast. Russell was sure that they'd be up at dawn, busy on their feet as the sun peaked over the horizon, illuminating the steady swells of water.He stayed there, trying to picture the scene, until the music came to life—he almost jumped when the chorus to a Police song came wailing from the defunct speakers.

The older men hardly budged; they were carved in stone and sat smoking, one of them talking now, but in such a low rasp that Russell could only imagine his mouth moving. He thought about leaving, pushed his bottle across the bar and riffled through his pockets for a few dollars. He was about to give up when he turned and saw his man across the room, and he wasn't alone. Dickerson was shabbily dressed, his long hair visible beneath a hooded sweatshirt. But the girl with him wore a short sun dress and combat boots—both accentuated her long, white legs.

She towered above Dickerson even though she was probably half his age. They were drunk, stumbling around by the pool tables, spilling a pitcher of beer on the floor as they tried to fill glasses, and Russell tried to size up the situation from a far.

The song ended and a reggae track took over the room, echoing bass in a dizzying fashion. He'd readied himself to walk over when he noticed the girl's face, and especially her tattoos. She had full sleeves of color covering both arms above the elbows and a pair of black wings that rose from beneath the tiny straps of her dress. Before he had a chance to think she looked up and caught him staring. He lost track of where he was for an instant and remembered, and at that moment he knew that he needed to get out of there. But it was too late: she'd made him. Dickerson was oblivious, head down, but she'd made him. If he wanted his money he'd have to deal with them both.

The song changed again to something he didn't recognize, a jazz number, and he grabbed a beer and made his way over. Dickerson leaned against the wall chalking a pool stick. A stack of quarters rested on the edge of the table. The girl still hadn't stopped watching him and Russell walked right up and sat down. She had black hair and a pale face; the tattoos on her arms were so full of color that they seemed to jump from the surface of her skin.

"Hey," she said. "Long time." Then she laughed, tilting her head back to show her neck.

The veins stood out on her throat like whipcord. Dickerson continued to work the stick. He stumbled a bit as he put down the chalk and Russell noticed he was shorter than he remembered, and that his teeth were rotten.

"Yeah," he answered, staring at the girl. "Long time." He held his bottle between two fingers. Either Dickerson hadn't noticed or he didn't care, but the girl knew him, and Russell now remembered their night together. In addition to the sleeves, she had a mess of smaller tattoos across her lower back that fused with the wings in a massive cross-hatch of black ink. At first she'd been embarrassed to take off her clothes. She'd said some days the tattoos felt like scars. But they were loaded that night, up past dawn, and after a while none of that mattered. It had been a few years and now he couldn't even recall her name. She might have been one of his sister's friends, and seeing her made him feel guilty again for leaving, but also silly for not going far enough away.

"This is Jed Dickerson," she said. "He lives by the pier." She reached for him but he was busy circling the table. He bent to feed quarters into the slots and fell to one knee, balancing himself with the pool cue. His eyes darted up quickly and Russell thought he saw a grin, but he didn't say anything or offer to shake.

"Jed, this is Snickers," she said. "He's an old friend."

They played a game of pool, her and Dickerson, a sloppy game that ended in laughter and more spilt beer. Dickerson still hadn't acknowledged him and Russell felt trapped, but he didn't want to leave without the money. So he watched, trying to recall the girl's name, wondering about the storm. He kept an eye on the clock though he had nowhere to go.

She was pretty, but he didn't think he wanted her again. When she laughed, her voice broke, and the laugh carried through the room, at once too loud and hoarse. She made a show of embracing her man whenever she could get him steady on his feet, and she made sure his hands were on her, that everyone knew the score. After a long game she set the rack, bending over the table so that the backs of her legs flashed through the dreary bar. Then she asked Russell if he wanted to play.

"I'm fine," he said. "Thanks."

"Play one, man." It was Dickerson. He was slouched over a little, showing his teeth. But he looked more alert, as if he'd adjusted somewhat to the bar and the booze and the situation, and the look on his face was undeniable. "Just one," he said. "Then you can take your ass home."

Russell squared him up: he'd taken off the hoodie and wore a plain white T-shirt. His arms were tan and strong and he had tattoos as well. But they were dull, washed out and hardly recognizable, as if they'd been acquired years before: now they looked like oil stains along his heavy forearms.

"OK," Russell said. "I'll play one." He grabbed a stick and set to break while Dickerson pulled out a wad of bills. As he dropped them on the table Russell decided that he looked drunk enough, but something else too. There was a slight tremor about him, in his hands and face.

Russell knew that he would indeed play one, but he could not let the man win.

She watched in silence. The music had stopped and the bar

felt like a museum, still but for their movements around the table. Russell could tell Dickerson was concentrating, taking his time with the shots. But it didn't matter—his hands were fluttering and he had to squint to see the cue ball. It would be hard to lose this game, but maybe harder to collect the money without incident. Instead of worrying he drank the rest of his beer and stole glances at the girl.

A few people walked into the bar—another cluster of guys—and the noise turned their heads. Dickerson went right for them, carrying the empty pitcher in his hand like a hammer. He greeted them loudly and it was obvious that they knew each other. The girl walked past Russell on the way to the bathroom. She smirked, shook her head slightly, but Russell couldn't tell if she was trying to call him out or if she was flirting.

"We're playing pool," Dickerson yelled from the bar. "Big money game." He made sure to check Russell's reaction. But he didn't return right away. Instead, he followed the girl down the hall, two of the guys in tow. The other two stood across the room and watched Russell, not smiling, not moving. They just watched. He couldn't tell what they were about but they looked local, more like bikers than surfers, and he wondered if they would even let him leave.

Instead, he finished the game alone, hitting in the rest of his balls. Then he shot Dickerson's. They went in easy, and he circled the table, avoiding the messy stack of bills balanced on the rail. When he'd hung his stick on the wall the girl was back, staring at him in silence. Her face was flushed, her eyes watery, and she was breathing through her mouth. "Hey," she said. "I saw your sister last night."

He heard himself answer, but he wasn't sure if she was finished. He didn't want to talk about his sister. He didn't even want to leave, though he knew it was the best idea. They stood for a moment, silent, until she tried to take a step and fell.

He leaned over her, lifted her head. She was coughing, spit flying as her body jerked forward. "Take me home," she whispered.

TRACHODON

"Let's go." From her knees, she reached for the money, stuffed the wad down the front of her dress so that it created a bulge between her breasts.

Russell didn't move to stop her. He knew she was drunk, probably more. Instead he got her to her feet and leaned her against the pool table.

"Snickers," she said. Her face was a mess of red, the skin around her eyes raw and hard.

"He asked me if I liked you." Her breathing was heavy and her eyes were closed. She lurched forward again, and he held her steady. He wanted to tell her that he was Russell now, things were different. He wanted to touch her face and tell her, but he still couldn't remember her name, and she was crying a little as she tried to speak.

"I told him no," she said. "That I didn't like you." She looked hurt, as if he'd started all this, dragged her down this road and forced her hand. Russell waited for her to cry, but she didn't. Instead she looked him dead in the eyes.

"But he asked me if I screwed you," she said, and as she did, she smiled and pulled away from him, adjusting the dress so the bulge disappeared. "And I said yes."

Before Russell had time to get angry, Dickerson was back. His boys were nowhere to be found. It was hard to tell if they were all in the bathroom now, doing lines of coke, or if they were outside waiting in the alley. "Buddy," he said. "Let's go." He glanced at the table and grabbed the girl by the arm. They marched toward the door and stopped as Dickerson looked back. "Let's go," he said again, and Russell followed.

Outside, there were stars but no moon. They walked to the ocean, passing stragglers along the way. The night was relatively quiet and Russell walked a few paces behind. Dickerson held the girl as she stumbled, slurring her words, weeping some and forcing them to stop every so often as she whispered something indecipherable. Dickerson seemed to find this funny, and he'd turn to Russell each time and nod. His smile said: "See this? Do you see this?" Then they'd lurch forward, making steady progress on the road to the beach.

There was no sign of the others from the bar and Russell felt a little disappointed. It was one thing to get a beating from a group of bikers, but this was something else entirely. Up ahead the sky glowed, a few clouds thrown over the starlight like thin blankets. They weren't storm clouds, they were just passing by on their way down the coast. If there was a storm without a name out there in the ocean, it was hundreds of miles away still, banking its way through the sea at a slow but steady clip.

When they reached the shore, Dickerson stopped. He dropped the girl in the sand and she cried a bit, her hands covering her face. He unzipped his pants and pissed into the dune, not far from her head. Russell watched and waited. The air was warm and the wind had died down. It was a beautiful night and he thought about how the beach ran in a crooked line up the coast, how you could walk for days, weeks even, and not even know where you were as you moved from state to state until it disappeared underfoot.

He felt a hand on his shoulder and noticed that Dickerson had a knife. His pants were still unzipped but he had a knife in his hand. The girl cried in the darkness, but it was quieter now, subdued, and Dickerson seemed to be speaking to her out of the corner of his mouth. Soon she would stop, Russell thought, sleep it off. Wake without memory. He wanted to picture her naked beneath the sheets, pulling this man close, touching his face where the stubble grew in gray-brown patches. If he did live by the pier, they might grab coffee after, take the cups down to the sea wall. There was a place where you could dip your feet in the surf and watch the waves while the fish swam below in frenzied circles, avoiding the pull of the tides. Sometimes they'd even nibble at your toes, hoping you were food.

Dickerson let go of Russell's shoulder and gestured with the knife, saying something, but Russell didn't hear. Instead, he watched Dickerson for a sign, thinking that together they were hugging the shore, caught between day and night. In a few hours people would be rolling out of bed for their lawn jobs and work on the roofs. There was plenty of work to be done and this made Russell a little sad, the endless string of things that needed attending. Dickerson held the knife but Russell could see that it was just a fishing knife, the blade was rusty, the tip broken off.

Dickerson didn't come forward. His mouth still moved, but he seemed more exhausted than angry. He looked like an old man and Russell hardly paid attention. He couldn't; his head ached from the beer and this scene seemed like something out of a movie, so out of focus in the weak light.

Russell wanted to think about the nameless storm instead, stranded out over the sea, but at this moment he couldn't do that either. Try as he might, he couldn't picture a mess of wind and rain, a funnel of air traveling across the surface of the water. It seemed impossible, and the impossibility disappointed him. It was as if the storm didn't exist—had never existed—and he turned away from the man with the knife and his crying girlfriend and started home, considering all this. As he walked, he thought he heard Dickerson finally say something out loud in the dark but he didn't stop to listen, he didn't slow his pace at all.

Horse and Trailer—Houma, LA

Katey Schultz

Bare Bones: On Landscape
and Influence

This winter I spent a month in the high desert foothills of Wyoming's Bighorn Mountains. Cloistered with five other artists on 1,000 acres owned by the Jentel Foundation, I got to thinking about the ways artists in different mediums are influenced by a drastic change in topography.

As a writer, my first point of influence is always specificity of language: buffalo jump, gumbo, bull pen. These words took on a vivid luster after weeks of scanning the snow-covered hillsides of Sheridan County. Likewise, the color palate of an early winter landscape caught my attention. Burnt yellow clusters of native grasses jutted from snowdrifts. Baked shale highways and scoria back roads climbed across prairies in gray and red lines. The poet among us described her experience as seasonally dependent. During an especially cold November, the vastness of "The West" was secondary to her experience of cabin fever. Many days, her landscape shrunk to the size of her studio and bedroom. Writing fireside beneath a warm blanket, her poetry employed a more self-reflective tone and used word play that mirrored the hunkered down evenings of single-digit temperatures and wine amongst friends.

The photographer of the group had a distinctly different approach. She began, interestingly enough, with narrative. Our location just five miles from the site of the 1866 Fetterman Fight enabled her to focus her research. She walked the staging areas of the battlefield and interviewed a historian, conceiving a series of photographs to reveal what she described as "the empty presence" of a place that once nourished the Cheyenne, Sioux, and Arapahoe horse warriors waiting in ambush to protect the last great migratory grounds of the buffalo.

One painter hailed from south Texas and had a more visceral experience than any of us when he attempted to jog in minus seven-degree weather. He returned sheepish and shocked with his first case of frost nip. During our time together, he listened while I exclaimed about the "glowing yellow" sunsets or the "blue-gray" cloud cover. He overheard conversations about the "bloodiest" massacre in the West or his fellow artists' debates against art interpretation. His paintings weren't so much directly influenced by the land, as was his auditory process for assimilating information. Echoes of this eavesdropping trickled into his work. The other painter, who hailed from the dense evergreen forests surrounding Spokane, Washington, described an immediate shift in her work. "I'm conceiving of everything in terms of space now. Before, I kept thinking in terms of line," she told me. Without even realizing it, she had stapled canvas and Mylar to her studio walls higher than eye level, forcing herself to reach and stretch as she painted.

The printmaker hand printed from woodcuts, a technique that requires carving to create positive and negative surfaces. "The process for carving is aggressive and so is the landscape here," she said. "Make a wrong cut and there's no going back. I think the extreme nature of Wyoming ignites that interest for me—its history of loss and gain, of trial and error, of lessons learned." Yet in both her work and the surrounding landscape, a comforting subtlety is evident. Well-craft woodcuts exhibit a gentle touch. In the right light, even the coldest day in the high desert can appear welcoming.

For each artist, the common denominator was time—time spent walking the land, time spent researching its stories, time spent looking or listening closely. Author Barry Lopez, whose work explores the relationship between landscape and culture, edited a creative dictionary of regional terms titled *Home Ground: Language for an American Landscape*. In his introduction, he writes:

To hear the unembodied call of a place, that numinous voice, one has to wait for it to speak through the harmony of its features—the soughing of the wind across it, its upward reach against a clear night sky, its fragrance after a rain. One must wait for the moment when the thing— the hill, the tarn, the lunette, the kiss tank, the caliche flat, the bajada—ceases to be a thing and becomes something that knows we are there.

If time spent is the primary method for being influenced by topography, then according to Lopez, the result is assimilation. The writer composes a story or poem that evokes the landscape through word choice and form. The photographer uses physical setting to convey the passage of time and the lure of absence. The visual artists mix a new batch of color or attend to a different tonal line.

The romantic in me wants to believe that the Bighorn Mountains knew all six of us were there, nestled in our studios, working the hours away. But what I find more convincing is the notion that assimilation happens with the art itself. As the last word is written or the final photograph framed, maybe for a brief moment an artist—in any medium—experiences the dissolution of ego, a moment perhaps as vast and inspiring as Wyoming's big sky country.

CONTRIBUTOR BIOGRAPHIES

Shane Darwent was born in Austin, TX and raised in Charleston, SC. He attended Maryland Institute College of Art in Baltimore where he received his BFA in printmaking and photography. Darwent currently lives in Chattanooga, TN where he is a photographer, sculptor, and freelance woodworker. Follow Shane's adventures on his blog, blackcameracrusades.blogspot.com.

Michael Delp is a writer of poetry, fiction, and nonfiction whose works have appeared in numerous national publications. He is the author of *Over the Graves of Horses* (Wayne State University Press, 1989), *Under the Influence of Water* (Wayne State University Press, 1997), and *The Last Good Water* (Wayne State University Press, 2003), in addition to six chapbooks of poetry. He teaches creative writing at the Interlochen Arts Academy and has received several awards for his teaching.

Nathan Graziano lives in Manchester, NH with his wife and two children. A high school English teacher, he recently completed his MFA at the University of New Hampshire. He is the author of *After the Honeymoon* (sunnyoutside, 2009), *Teaching Metaphors* (sunnyoutside, 2007), *Not So Profound* (Green Bean Press, 2004), *Frostbite* (GBP, 2002) and seven chapbooks of poetry and fiction. His work has appeared in *Rattle, Night Train, Word Riot, Sententia, Freight Stories, The Coe Review, The Owen Wister Review,* and others. For more information, visit his website: www.nathangraziano.com or blog: www.nathangraziano.blogspot.com.

Shannon Huffman Polson is a native Alaskan living with her husband and son between a home in Seattle and their cabin in Denali. Shannon contributed to *More Than 85 Broads*, has published in *Seattle Magazine, Alaska Magazine*, and is working on a book about a 2006 trip to the Arctic. Visit www.aborderlife.com and www.theultimathule.org.

Brian Maxwell is a graduate student instructor at University of North Dakota, studying literature and creative writing. His stories have appeared in *Fugue, Evansville Review, Beloit Fiction Journal, Silk Road, Permafrost, Louisville Review, Red Rock Review,* and *South Dakota Review.* Recently, his work has been translated and will appear in the Italian anthology *Empty Sockets,* published by Intermezzo Press.

Abby E. Murray has an MFA from Pacific University and currently teaches creative writing in Colorado Springs. Her poetry has been published in recent issues of *War Literature & the Arts, CALYX,* and *Court Green,* and her first chapbook (*Me and Coyote*) was selected for publication by Marvin Bell in the 2010 Lost Horse Press *New Poets / Short Books* series. She lives with her husband, two cats (Suvi and Lunchbox) and an unruly dog named Flynn. Her website is www.abbyemurray.com, with the poetry link www.abbyemurray.blogspot.com.

Scott Nadelson is the author of two story collections: *Saving Stanley: The Brickman Stories,* winner of the Oregon Book Award for short fiction and the Great Lakes Colleges Association New Writers Award; and *The Cantor's Daughter,* recipient of the Reform Judaism Fiction Prize. His work has recently appeared in *Ploughshares, Glimmer Train, Alaska Quarterly Review,* and *Post Road,* and his new story collection, *Aftermath,* is forthcoming from Hawthorne Books in fall 2011. Visit www.scottnadelson.com.

TRACHODON MAGAZINE
AVAILABLE AS MULTI-FORMAT EBOOKS

- Available for all popular devices including Kindle, Nook, Kobo, smartphones, and iPad.
- Instantly available—no more waiting for shipping dates!
- Same content— expanded web links to our contributors.
- Saves paper!
- Lower cost!

**www.trachodon.org
for more details**

Advertise in TRACHODON

Full Page	1/2 Page	1/4 Page
4.5 x 7	4.5 x 3.5/2.25 x 7	3.5 x 2.25
1 Issue: $100	1 Issue: $60	1 Issue: $35
2 Issues: $180	2 Issues: $110	2 Issues: $65

TRACHODON: a dinosaur of a little magazine

Name_____

Address_____

City_____

State_____Zip_____

Email_____

[ ] 1-year subscription (2 issues) for $18.00
[ ] Single issue/sample copy for $10.00
Use our online system at www.trachodon.org or enclose a check payable to
Trachodon Publishing LLC and mail to:

TRACHODON
PO Box 1468
Saint Helens, OR 97051

TRACHODON: a dinosaur of a little magazine

Name_____

Address_____

City_____

State_____Zip_____

Email_____

[ ] 1-year subscription (2 issues) for $18.00
[ ] Single issue/sample copy for $10.00
Use our online system at www.trachodon.org or enclose a check payable to
Trachodon Publishing LLC and mail to:

TRACHODON
PO Box 1468
Saint Helens, OR 97051